THE EPOCALYPSE

THE EPOCALYPSE

Economy Crisis and Collapse

By Dr. Niaz Ahmad Khan F.R.C.S., PhD.

PARTRIDGE

To order additional copies of this book, contact
Toll Free 800 101 2657 (Singapore)
Toll Free 1 800 81 7340 (Malaysia)
orders.singapore@partridgepublishing.com

www.partridgepublishing.com/singapore

Presentation

HOW TO RESTORE THE US ECONOMY

MBBS
MUTUAL BENEFIT BOND SYSTEM

A Perfect solution for USA to get out of all Financial crisis in just matter of Days

Dr Niaz Ahmed Khan
FRCS ,PhD

Recession Reversed?

Recession will not only be stopped but will be reversed In just

30 days !

Massive Employment Opportunities!

At Least **20** million people employed within **30** days with zero cost to the government.

No Taxes, No Duties ?

All kinds of Taxes removed but duties slashed to **1/10** %

Duties 1/10 %

Annual Budget Collection in 24 hours!

Zero debt

State collects more than a year budget within **24** hours and much more after **30** days .

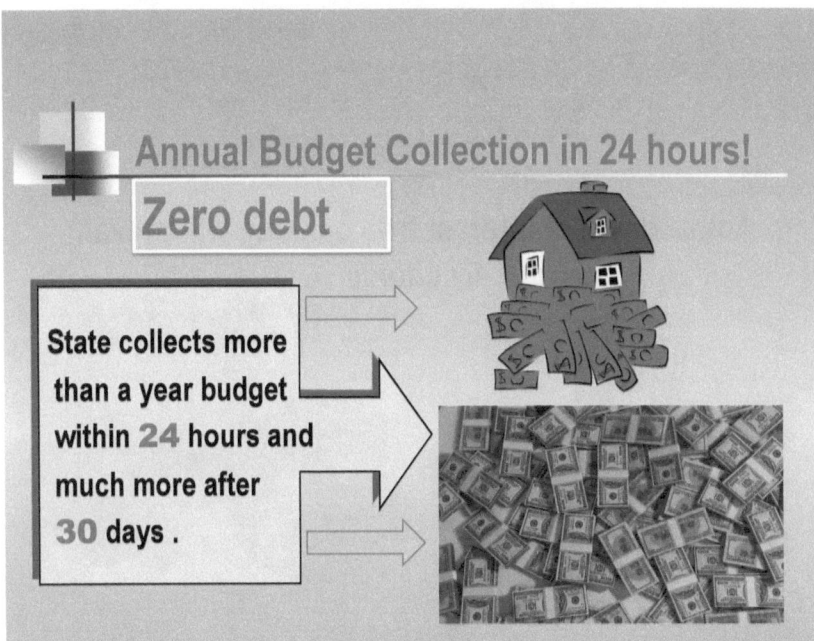

Production Cost Drops to more than **50%**

Cost of production in all sectors will be reduced to more than **50%** and hence the cost of living will also be tremendously reduced for every person .

Interest Free Banking!

A new dawn of interest free banking will prevail by choice

Interest

0%

Goodbye to Poverty!

End of Poverty and capitalistic system with the replacement of a new incentive based system.

POVERTY

0

Zero Expense !!!

" 0 "
Expense
to the state by
implementing
this system

True Or False?

One's gain is other man's loss
is not always true

Government and Public both are winners

 +

My Claims?

- Prove these claims wrong and win

10 Million Dollars !

The Miracle?

?

How this Miracle will happen ?

MBBS system

Interest Free Bonds!

State will float Interest Free Bonds in the form of smart debt cards with pin code that can be used by rich and poor alike, bonds will be replacing dollar but only in government sector and at least 15 % bonds will also be used in private sector

Conditions?

Conditions applying to sell the Bonds

In the First 30 Days

State will sell bonds in the first 30 days at the rate of 5 bond per dollar .

(but at least 50,000 dollar or multiple of it will get this rate.) This is an investment with at least 100 percent Return within 30 days.

In the Next 30 days

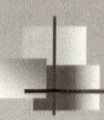

In the next 30 days
the rate will be 4 Per dollar
but the rate of 3 will apply
for the rest of the year for
 the same amount.

Balance Sheet

The state gains at least 3.75 to 5 trillion dollar in 24 hours and much more after 30 days and sky is the limit after one year as no body wants to be left out after seeing these incredible incentives .

The total loss to the state can not be more than the annual budget by removing all kind of taxes and duties .

Why Private Sector will buy Bonds?

To get 60% discount on everything in government sector

The Grand prize draw everyday.

Business incentives

100% return in 30 days

Daily Draw of One Billion Dollar!

1000 Prizes of 1 million dollar everyday from the bonds bought by the public

1 Billion Dollar per Day

Use of Bonds in Government Sector!

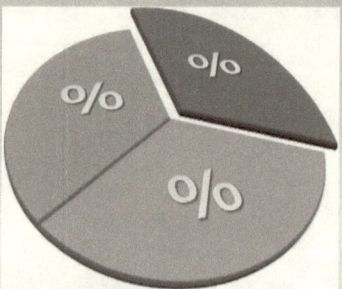

%

%

%

At least 15 % bonds will replace dollar in Private sector as well

Advantages of Bonds ! Example

Bonds will be used
in Government sector
where commodities
and services
state is providing.
(If the rate is
5 bonds per dollar)

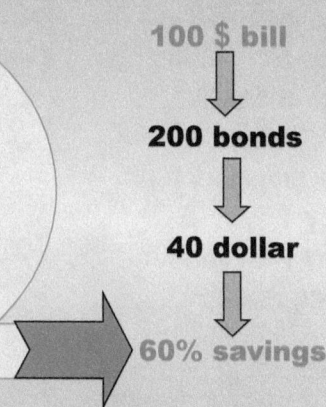

100 $ bill
↓
200 bonds
↓
40 dollar
↓
60% savings

Who will Sell the Bonds?

All poor and unemployed
persons will be employed
on 10% commission but no
salary with a yearly quota
of 3 million. This quota
can be sold in a day or one
month or in one
year.(USMF will employ at
least 20 million agents)

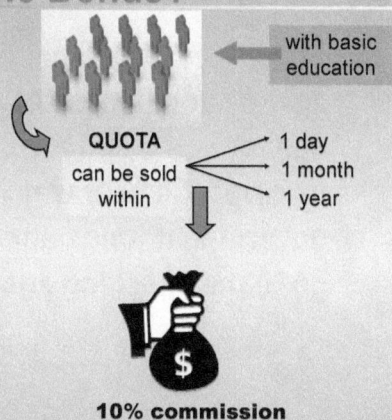

with basic
education

QUOTA
can be sold
within

1 day
1 month
1 year

10% commission

Who will Employ the Agents?

Government will ask for bids from reputable organizations like banks. Lowest bid will form a monetary fund agency. 2nd, 3rd & 4th bidders will form the auditing teams.

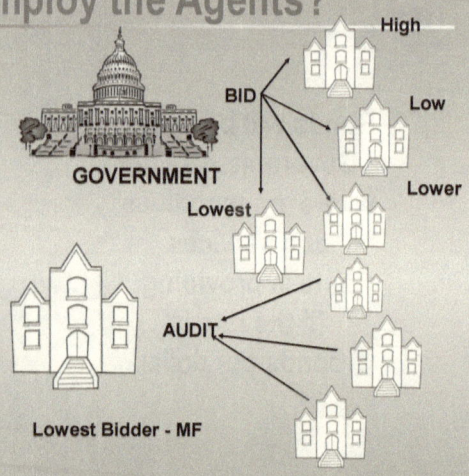

GOVERNMENT

BID

High

Low

Lower

Lowest

AUDIT

Lowest Bidder - MF

Checking of monetary fund Agency

These teams will check the monetary fund agency and in case of any mistake or fraud, agency will be fined 10 times the amount involved. 50 % of which will go to the government funds and rest of the 50% will go to the checking agencies accounts .

Agent to Pay!

Every agent will pay 500 dollar for one year registration to monetary agency to build the infrastructure . The QUOTA will become half if the agent can not afford 500 dollar .

100 % return in 30 days

How ?

Bond agents will be compelled to sell their yearly quota as quickly as possible by offering the investors the discount in commission say 5 %.

1st Flood Gate!

At least **25%** people will invest **50,000** dollar or multiple of it, so the result will be **3.75** trillion dollar. State collects this amount within 24 hours. This is not a debt so there is no interest involved.

| 25%-75,000,000 | = | 3.75 trillion dollar |

Why?

Because nobody wants to be left out after seeing these incredible incentives.

2nd Flood Gate!

At least another **25 %** of the population will join this race by selling gold or taking loan from the banks . The state will collect approximately 3.75 trillion dollar once the investor sells his quota near 5 per dollar without the condition of amount involved .

3rd Flood Gate

Government investment share

Now all the private sector money has gone into state account and the banks are worried. But the government will provide 80 % interest free liquidity on profit and loss sharing basis. Government will get 40 % of the profit and the banks will share 60 %. In this way the banks will be more than happy to receive the interest free money with much more margin of profit than the interest based banking . Imagine ,how much money government will get?

Profit and loss arrangement

Now the state is in the driving seat and has become a master lender and not the borrower from the banks . State will guarantee the existing loans by the banks but the choice will be given to the banks to become partner in the new system or continue the old one. The state's 80 % Liquidity will not be given on interest at any cost but will share in profit and loss arrangement. The banks will receive 60% of profit and the state will have 40% . The amount government will receive in profit cannot be imagined .

Duty free option

10,000 dollar will exempt **10 million** duty and this option will be available for first one month only and this option has to be used in one year but this duty free option can be sold partly or as a whole. This will kick start the economy in a tremendous way as there will be more than few thousands big, medium and small new industries with in a year resulting in millions of new job. The only loss to state is the revenue generated in one year from the present duty which will have no comparison to what the state will achieve in one month through this new option.

4th Flood Gate!

By the end of 30 days the state is expected to announce a tax free country, now all the money is white creating a big jump to the economy because the black money will end up in the government accounts as no question will be asked regarding the source of money when all kinds of taxes are removed.

Mortgage and lease arrangement 1

State will provide **80** % liquidity for mortgage to the new home owners and the businesses after checking the feasibility . State will charge rent and not interest which will never be more than **2** % on decreasing scale as monthly installment will reduce the rent every month.

Registration Fee for Bonds !

 # Types of Registration fees & Benefits

5 Bonds for the whole Year !

Professionals and salaried persons pay 10,000 dollar at the start of the year and get the rate of 5 Bonds for the rest of the year.

Private Sector !

Private sector small time business pay 10,000 dollar yearly and get 20,000(double) new bonds at the rate of 5 every month.

(provided the business collects 10,000 bonds to get it replaced from the agency free of charge for issuing new bonds)

Gold Mine No.1

Registration fee for industries !

Paying 50,000 $ will entitle the business to sell its products through the already selected agency by bids . Business will get 5 bond per dollar or duty free option equal to the amount sold through the agency.

Terms !

1- Business will have to surrendered 15% bonds at each sale to the agency who will deposit these bonds in government accounts.

2- The amount sold through the agency will be 10 times of the registration fee and not more unless the registration fee is increased .

Gold Mine No.2

The Benefits !

Everything Sold through this agency benefits the business by getting cheap bonds and duty free throughout the year.

Gold Mine  **No.3**

A Category 3 business cannot invest billions of dollar needed to buy cheap bonds at the beginning of a financial year, so they would have to sell their products through the agency to get cheap bonds or duty free option .

Gold Mine  **No.4**

Rush to Sell !

Every Business will Sell all its goods or even more to get registration fee back by selling the extra bonds or duty free option in the open market.

Gold Mine **No.5**

If the total daily transactions across the country is **10** trillion $ then by the Gold Mine option 3% (**15 %** bonds) of **10** trillion will be **300** billion $ everyday credited into Govt.'s account without any compulsion.

So if **300** US $ daily , then the calculation will be **9** trillion dollar in One Month

and in **1** year

9 Trillion Dollar x12 =108 Trillion $

GST or VAT , bad dream of the Past

Now every business man or a production house will sell their goods through the agency ,so that they can get cheap bonds or duty free option through out the year and will also make profit on the registration fee paid to the state by selling the extra bonds or duty free option in the open market .

Goods and Services Tax

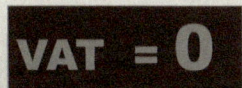

VAT = 0

Services & commodities already Privatized

All these services will remain in the private hands but without VAT ,GST ,Tax and Duty . This will bring the prices of all the services to 1/3 of its present cost and will make a big relief for the masses .

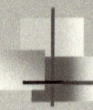

How the bonds will attract the private sector -1

Businesses will be forced to sell the products through the monetary agency as this is the only way to get cheep bonds or duty free option on payment of 15 % bonds at each transaction. The business will also try to make profit or at least recover the registration fee by selling the end product cheaper to the dealer or sub dealer after accepting at least 15 % bonds and the dealer will do the same with the sub dealer or the ultimate shop keeper. The shop keeper will ask for at least the same amount of bonds from the customer by lowering the cash price in dollar which the customer will readily accept because of much cheaper cash price.

How the bonds will attract the private sector -2

In the retail section the competition will be intense by accepting more bonds and thus reducing the cash price. This ratio of accepting bonds can easily reach 40 % or even 100 % in some rare cases. Small businesses will have to collect at least same amount of bonds if not more to get cheap bonds every month which is double the amount of registration fee. This is a big incentive to accept maximum bonds and reduce his cost price and increase the profit margin .Retailer not accepting bonds at the time of sale will go out of business in no time.

All nationalities invited

As there is no restriction in buying bonds by any nationality, it will give a tremendous boost to the economy of the country. Approximately 65 million visitors every year will add at least another 3.3 trillion dollar to the government funds .

Till debt do us part

Total US debt (public and External) is 59 Trillion $ which is equivalent to $190,000 per capita, or $760,000 per family of 4. If we include several un-funded liabilities then total debt (private plus government) is $156.5 Trillion ,equivalent to $508,117 per person which is equivalent to $2 million per family of 4. Each month government is printing 85 billion dollar as a stimulus. This is another debt which is increasing the total liabilities . National debt is increasing by 2.37 billion dollar per day.

(Source -Grandfather Economic Report series by Michael Hodges)

CONSIDER FAMOUS QUOTES

- *"No generation has a right to contract debts greater than can be paid off during the course of its own existence."*
  George Washington to James Madison 1789

- *"We hear sad complaints sometimes of merciless creditors; whilst the acts of merciless debtors are passed over in silence."* -
  William Frend, 1817

- *"I place economy among the first and most important virtues, and debt as the greatest of dangers to be feared."* - Thomas Jefferson"

CONSIDER FAMOUS QUOTES

- "There is no means of avoiding the final collapse
  of a boom brought about by credit (debt) expansion.
  The alternative is only whether the crisis should come sooner
  as the result of a voluntary abandonment of further credit (debt)
  expansion,
  or later as a final and total catastrophe of the currency system
  involved." - Ludwig von Misses

- *"The decline of great powers is caused by simple economic over
  extension." - by Paul Kennedy*

The killer whales

Tax ,interest and duties are the killer whales of
the capitalistic system .Slaughter these whales
and release the economy from the life long
imprisonment .Economy will fly like a free bird
and will achieve incredible new heights ,making
this world a true paradise on this earth where
there will be no poverty as poverty is the mother
of all evils .Seeing is believing.

Table of Contents

Reversing the World Recession Overnight

SUMMARY

Reversing the World Recession Overnight
A Method to Address Economic Recession, Remove Poverty, Terrorism, Improve Law and Order, Reduce Drug Abuse, Inflation And Taxes in an Interest Free Economy.

By: Dr. Niaz Ahmed Khan, FRCS, PhD

ABSTRACT:

I have developed a new financial instrument which will be much more valuable than the bonds or the treasury bills government sells on the open market to raise much needed funds to run the country. These are all interest based instruments and can only be used by institutions. The instrument I am proposing is without interest and will be used by everyone to purchase goods and services in the government and private sector resulting in discounts up to 60%. This is why these will be massively bought up front in large amounts in the shortest period of time, to run the country for at least a year and more by the end of the year.

SUMMARY OF THE BOOK:

The world is facing many challenges with no solution in sight. The main cause of all these ills is POVERTY.

Float bonds, which can be used by everybody rich or poor and are not debt to the state so there is no question of interest. *How*: Take the example of the USA, which is going through a great recession. The USA borrows money by selling treasury bills and the interest based bonds. The suggestion is to sell these bonds on a non interest basis.

1. Buying all goods and services under govt. control with these bonds and these bonds will replace the dollar.
2. **10 million dollar** Duty waved off.

3. **1 billion** dollar prize draw from the bonds bought by the public every day.
4. At least **100** percent return in one month.

EXAMPLE: ONE dollar buys five bonds on the condition that the amount should be $50,000 or a multiple of it. Fewer amounts will get the rate of four and three. This massive discount period is only for first month at the start of the implementation of this system. In the second month, the rate will be four, but the rate of three will apply to subsequent months for the same amount.

WHERE WILL THESE BONDS BE USED?

All state controlled services and commodities. *EXAMPLE*: A bill of (any service or Commodity) $100 can be paid with 200 bonds and there will be no exception to this rule. A simple formula will apply: Total bill in dollars x2 is the number of bonds surrendered. The price in bonds will not be less than the cost price, but without the direct indirect taxes and the duties, which are added to the present cost to make it very expensive. It will attract at least 50 million people to take this opportunity as early as possible. If one is sure of making 100% profit within thirty days, there will be many more that will help themselves.

RESULT

The government gets at least $2.5 trillion within twenty-four hours and much more during the rest of the year. THIS IS NOT A DEBT AS STATE HAS SOLD BONDS (Commodity) WHICH IS AN ALTERNATE CURRENCY AND DO NOT CARRY ANY INTEREST. One immediately thinks, who will bear the loss and this loss to the state will not be more than total year budget of $2.5 trillion, which it collects in one year with all the taxes and the duties. The bond price is simply a cost price without any kind of tax or duty. So there is a net gain of approximately 2.5 trillion within a short period of time. **THE first floodgate** of money has been opened.

WHO WILL SELL THESE BONDS?

The state will float tenders to select a private agency (USMF) (UNITED STATES MONITORY FUND JUST A NAME GIVEN TO THIS ORGANIZATION) with the lowest bid WHERE the second, third and fourth bidders will be auditors of the USMF. This agency will employ at least 20 million unemployed on a 10% commission basis and without any salary. These agents will have to pay $500 as an annual fee to USMF in order to build the infrastructure for the sale of bonds. The agents' quota will be $300,000 per month. They will be allowed to sell their whole yearly quota in one day or in a month. This will only materialize if the agent shares his commission with the buyer. The greater the share of commission, the quicker the sale. The investor or a buyer will sell these bonds at the same rate of five per dollar and his bonds will sell like hot cakes every day, as there is no condition of the amount of money to purchase the bonds. In this way, even the poorest person will get the same or near the same rate as the investor earns a profit from the commission, which he takes from the agent and makes almost 100% profit by only investing $50,000. He will sell these bonds repeatedly and will keep almost 6% of the profit, every day, until the demand subsides. NOW THINK HOW MUCH MONEY THE STATE HAS ACCUMULATED. Much more than few years budget in matter of only one month.

THE FLOOD GATES OF MONEY AND THE TURNING POINT

This is the *second floodgate* of money and there are still four more floodgates of money yet to open. So at the end of thirty days or even much earlier, the government declares that the country will be tax-free forever. With the removal of all kinds of direct and indirect taxes and duties the price of oil, electricity, telephone and of all other services under government control is now almost 60% less than before, as these are being purchased by bonds (which is the cost price) and not with dollars. The production cost of everything has come down tremendously.

SECOND OPTION

STATE ALSO OFFERS A TEN MILLION DOLLAR DUTY FREE IF ONE DEPOSITS $100,000 NON REFUNDABLE. THIS BRINGS OUT ALL THE BLACK AND SPARE MONEY, WHICH THE STATE

WAS NOT ABLE TO GET BEFORE AND AS THERE IS NO TAX AND HENCE NO TAX EVASION SO ALL THE MONEY IS WHITE AS IT IS BEING GIVEN TO GOVERNMENT.

This is the ***third floodgate*** of money, which is even bigger than the first one and the exact amount is impossible to asses unless the system is implemented. In order to provide cheap bonds throughout the year government offers three types of registration fees.

1. Pay $10,000 at the start of the year and get the rate of five for the rest of the year. This will suit the professionals and salaried person.
2. Pay $10,000 yearly and get 20,000 new bonds at the rate 5 every month, but one has to collect 10,000 bonds (equal to the fee) to get this cheap rate throughout the year. The higher the registration fee, the more the entitlement of cheap bonds. This registration will suit any small time business who will sell his product cheaper, provided 15% bonds are also paid with the rest of the cash by the customer. (SEE THE NEXT REGISTRATION FOR FURTHER EXPLANATION OF 15% BONDS.) This will apply to all goods in the private sector and does not apply to the government sector. This is a big incentive to accept bonds in the private sector, as the business accepting more bonds will have more business than the trader not accepting bonds. The bonds market will multiply and there will be a constant need for bonds in the open market.
3. The third type of registration will cost $50,000, which will entitle the business to sell its products through the USMF. The value of merchandise sold through this source will help the business to get the five bond per dollar rate or opt for the duty free option equal the amount sold. But with the one condition of surrendering 15% bonds of each sale in dollars.

EXAMPLE:

MERCHANDISED SOLD THROUGH USMF $1000. BONDS SURRENDERED 150 ARE DEPOSITED IN STATE ACCOUNT TO BE SOLD AGAIN SO THE CYCLE OF BONDS IS ESTABLISHED.

A receipt of bonds surrendered is obtained from USMF for evidence of sale of merchandise and this receipt will entitle the traders to get cheap bonds or the duty free option throughout the year BUT THE SAME RECEIPT CAN BE USED ONCE ONLY.

WHAT IS THE BENEFIT TO BUSINESS?

Now all the business will opt for this registration in order to reduce the cost of production. The 15% of bonds the business will get back through a chain of dealers, sub dealers and ultimately the customer will pay this bond portion as he will get the end product very cheap because of the tremendous cut in the cost of production by the factors already mentioned. This will replace the GST or the VAT or the two price system seen all over USA. Almost everybody will sell their product through this channel, as it will be much more costly to sell the product outside this system, as cheap bonds are not available otherwise.

According to rough estimate, at least $ 100 trillion in transactions are carried out every day in the US and at each transaction 15% bonds are being surrendered. The price for fifteen bonds is $3. So 3% of 100 trillion will be $300 billion which goes into a government account without any compulsion every day (UNBELIEVABLE). This is the *fourth floodgate* of money AND IS CALLED **THE GOLD MINE**. Now the state is sitting in the drivers seat and all the money in the banks of the private sector have been transferred into government accounts. Banks are no more the lenders, but are the borrower from the state, which is the only source left and will invest in business with sound feasibility and study checked by the state bank. The state will offer to invest 80% and the bank will bring investors who are willing to pool the remaining 20%. This 20% will be deposited in the bank and the bank will oversee the business. Running expenses will be given to the investor from its share of 20%. There will be no collateral and share of the profit and loss will be shared in the ratio of 60 and 40. The bank will share the 60% with the investor and 40% will go to state funds. The state will provide everything under its control below cost, which will further reduce the cost of production and at the same time will MARKEDLY improve the profit margins OF ALL THE BUSINESSES. No major business can refuse this offer. Any bank showing repeated loss, will go out of business as there will be no more funds available from the government and all other interest based sources would not be available any more. Interest based banking is gone forever or it may be at a very small scale. The state will offer CHEAP BONDS THROUGH OUT THE YEAR under the above mentioned conditions. THE DUTY FREE OPTION WILL HELP INDUSTRY. The quota which can be sold, is ten times the amount of Registration,. The amount of profit government will share will be unimaginable and this is the *fifth flood gate* opened.

THEN WHY NOT INVEST ON A PROFIT AND LOSS SHARING BASIS?

Last but not the least, the government will acquire all the land on lease without any force and will provide all the needs to the formers, THROUGH THE CORPORATE FARMING SECTOR HIRED BY THE STATE below cost and will become the shareholder according to the mutual contract with the land owner. This is the *sixth flood gate* of money opened.

DRUG ABUSE ELIMINATED

When all the possible land is being cultivated by the best agriculture engineers, there will be a much better yield and much more profit to land owner then who will not join hands with the government.

THE OBVIOUS BENEFIT WILL BE NO MORE POPPY CULTIVATION IN COUNTRIES WHICH ARE POOR AND LARGELY DEPEND ON THE POPPY CROP. NOW THERE IS NO MORE POPPY AND NO MORE DRUGS. All the above claims have been proved to be true except the terrorism.

HOW WILL TERRORISM BE ELIMINATED?

We have to look at root cause and it is POVERTY and NOT the religion, which is being falsely blamed. The going rate for a suicide bomber is $1,500 in Pakistan, Iraq and in Afghanistan. Can one believe that anyone having at least two meals a day would blow himself up? The countries where these attacks are happening are extremely poor and the extremist elements who themselves are or were poor, exploit these very same poor people to carry out attacks for money to save their families dying from hunger and this is an open secret. Extreme elements have large forces that are recruited from poor areas, as there are no jobs anywhere. They provide these raw recruits with only food and shelter and at same time brainwash them and train some of them to carry out these attacks by giving them enough money in their lives to support their dependents. You might mention a few isolated cases of being well-to-do and still carring out these attacks. Once poverty is removed in these areas by implementing this system, these attacks will come to an end immediately. This system is not only meant for the USA, but will be easily applicable to every country.

MY ANALYSIS AND PREDICTION ABOUT US ECONOMY

The U.S economy is like a giant oak tree that has rotten roots, hollow stems, and dying leaves, and it is quite possible that this mighty tree will fall and bury every nation relaxing under its shade. MBCS is the fertilizer that can bring the U.S. economic tree back to life.

This prediction is available on internet and written in a book entitled ISLAMIC ECONOMIC REVOLUTION OF THE CENTURY published in USA and UK in 2006.

A strong effort is being made to reach economic team of Barack Hussein Obama. But so far there has been no success. I have the blue print of real and practical solution to get US forces out of prosperous, peaceful and stable Iraq and Afghanistan without violence in matter of 6 months. If all the above impossible claims I have made are possible and true to the last detail then there is no reason that this message should not reach to the highest authority in the Barack Hussein Obama administration for their prompt future course of action.

CHAPTER ONE

INTRODUCTION

There is nothing certain but death and taxes. Since the earliest days of human history, governments have collected taxes. Ancient Chinese, Egyptian, Indian farmers and European feudal serfs paid tithes on their lands. With the rise of the middle classes, accountable governments have levied taxes on incomes, goods, capital, wealth, inheritance, and even windows. Although taxes are an inevitable part of life, societies have had to solve several problems associated with obtaining the money needed to run their governments and maintain their infrastructures: How much money to collect... How to collect it... Where to collect it... Who will collect it... and how to spend it. Some societies have used religion to guide their tax collection and laws. Other societies have used pragmatism and common sense to create the procedures for collecting taxes and establish laws.

While everyone pays taxes, ordinary, often poorer citizens who cannot pay for good tax advice carry the largest tax burden. From their ranks come the teachers, engineers, doctors, nurses, lawyers, scientists, and other high-value citizens without whom most societies would be so much poorer. It seems unfair that the people who contribute the most to a society's well-being are forced to carry the largest tax load. Modern-day people would be much better off if they lived in a tax-free society.

A world without taxes would be a paradise to many people, but it seems unimaginable, a pipe dream, an illusion. It seems an impossible dream to find a system that eliminates taxes; However, using the mutual benefit bond system (MBBS), it is possible to create a tax-free world. Although people may laugh at the idea of a tax-free world, many people also laughed at the idea of landing astronauts on the moon, splitting the atom, or curing diseases. Using MBBS, it is possible to…

1. Abolish all taxes.
2. Fund governments in new and productive ways.
3. Create incentives for rich and poor citizens.
4. Promote sensible public and private investment.
5. Make governments more accountable for spending.
6. Improve the quality of life for all people.
7. Eliminate poverty and illiteracy and the social ills caused by them.

Although MBBS seems like another fad, another 5-minute wonder, it is a system that can achieve this utopian ideal.

MBBS is based on incentive based principles, and it is designed to:
1. Eliminate unfair financial burdens from all sectors of society.
2. Remove taxes, duties, and levies.
3. Revolutionize government revenue collection and liquidity.
4. Eliminate poverty.
5. Rebuild national infrastructures.
6. Restore law and order.
7. Provide all citizens with equal opportunities.

This book describes MBBS and how it works. It discusses the weaknesses of the present taxation system and its adverse effect on the lives of billions of people. The World Bank and International Monetary Fund (IMF) and their effect on the economies of developing countries are examined. This book compares MBBS in the USA and the United Kingdom and present financial instruments.

There is a discussion about the role of the interest free banking system when MBBS is instituted, and a description of how different countries collect taxes. In addition, this book explains how MBBS can help eliminate the drug trade, terrorism, poverty, taxes and reverse recession in matter of days with a massive jump start in the economy of every country implementing this system.

CHAPTER TWO

MBBS (MUTUAL BENEFIT BOND SYSTEM) HOW MBBS WORKS: A CASE STUDY OF THE USA

MBBS is a simple system. In this system, all goods and services under government control are offered to end users and consumers at two prices. The first price is the current or prevailing market price and includes all types of taxes and duties a government collects to meet its budget requirements. This price is much higher than the price offered through MBBS and it includes most of the taxes and duties. The second price is much lower than the current market price, because it is offered at almost cost price by the government if purchased at the cheapest price (i.e., five bonds per dollar) and it also depends on the price of a MBBS bond. This lower price is the incentive for consumers and lower end users to participate in MBBS.

In order to obtain this lower price, the buyer has to pay for a commodity or service under government control with a certain number of MBBS bonds. The number of bonds will be shown on the bill provided by the government authority. In addition, the bill will also show the current prevailing price, which can be easily calculated by the purchaser because it will always be double the amount of bonds at the current price in dollars. For example, ten dollars is the present price, which can be paid in bonds in the form of two times bonds. The number of bonds will be two times the amount of dollars. Two prices are used in MBBS in order to calculate the bond price of a good or service. In addition, the current price is kept, because it shows how expensive a good or service would cost if a consumer decides not to use MBBS bonds. The savings

3

to the buyer can range from 20% to 60% or more, depending on the rate of bond. As a result, the consumer gets more for less.

In addition to lower prices, MBBS encourages buyers to participate in the scheme by offering discounts on bulk buys of bonds. As a result, a buyer can establish a price for a commodity or service by timing the purchase of bonds to take advantage of discounts. These discounts also include allowances for duty-free imports instead of cheap bonds or both. They are offered in the first, second, and third months of a financial year. After the discount period expires, the rate will be fixed for the rest of the year.

MBBS bonds would be available from a non-government organization (NGO) and its agents. The name of this agency will depend on the government. For example, in the USA, this agency could be called the United States Monetary Fund (USMF). Organizations would bid for the right to sell bonds and the agency selected to operate the monetary fund would employ agents who would receive a 10% commission on all bond sales. The organization with the lowest bid and the ability to put the scheme into operation in the shortest time, would receive the contract. The second-, third-, or fourth-lowest bidders as well as the government would audit the monetary fund. These auditors would work independently on a fixed fee paid by the monetary fund plus a 50% penalty imposed on USMF, which would be 10 times the amount of any discrepancy or fraud. The government would receive the remaining 50% of the penalty.

No rational business, organization or individual can afford to ignore this scheme if it is offered; therefore, it is reasonable to assume the following:

1. People, businesses, and organizations will purchase large quantities of bonds.
2. They will purchase them in the early part of the year in order to take advantage of discounts.
3. Bonds will be purchased for a number of reasons other than simply paying bills. For example, saving bonds, speculating in sales later in the year, and holding bonds as a hedge against unexpected expenses.

4. Bonds will be used at every opportunity to reduce the cost of producing goods and services from government imports to the point of sale to the end user.

This is like a lottery but without any cost to a person. These draws would encourage people to hold their bonds in the hopes of winning the draw. As a result, the government would have more money than expected because bonds are not being used. The government is not paying interest on them and they would not be recalled unless the value drops below a certain level. If the value drops below a certain level, the addition to lower costs, MBBS would include lucky draws everyday, which government would buy back the bonds at a low rate in order to increase the value of the bonds.

MBBS has a number of benefits for a government that is having problems collecting enough revenue to meet its needs:

1. At the beginning of each year, the monetary fund would offer MBBS bonds for sale without restriction. MBBS bonds would cover all government-controlled goods and services throughout the entire economic chain; therefore, there should be a large demand for these bonds. The cash raised by the sale of these bonds would go straight to the government through the monetary fund. In many developing countries, the initial sale of bonds will produce enough funds to cover the financial needs of a government for several years, because the underground economy will merge with the mainstream economy.

2. In this scheme, a government takes the lead in price reductions by discounting fuel, electricity, telephones, and so forth, which would reduce household, agricultural and industrial costs. This would have a significant, positive impact on economic activity, because a reduction in the prices of all essential goods and services with free imports would bring down factory prices and at the same time increase profitability. This will be an attractive incentive for new investment.

3. A government would benefit from increased liquidity, investment and economic activity. In addition, as the economy grows, the government would sell more bonds.
4. This new economy is attractive to all parties and people engaged in the black economy found in many developing countries will migrate to MBBS. It will no longer be attractive to work outside the system, because it will be impossible to compete with it on price.

MBBS is a unique, risk-free approach to raising revenue for governments. It does not require a government to give up its current system of revenue generation until MBBS proves that it is capable of raising enough money to meet a government's needs. Once the system is in place, it will transform dysfunctional economies often found in the developing world into open, transparent, free markets in which the government and citizens co-operate to drive prices down, create surplus budgets, and increase investment. Once a government has accumulated more than enough money to run the country for a year, it would announce a complete tax holiday in which no further income tax would be imposed on any person or businesses. This is the starting point for an industrial revolution.

MBBS in the Usa, A Case Study

According to the 2014 CIA World Fact book, The US has the largest and most technologically powerful economy in the world, with a per capita GDP of $49,800. In this market-oriented economy, private individuals and business firms make most of the decisions and the federal and state governments buy needed goods and services predominantly in the private marketplace. US business firms enjoy greater flexibility than their counterparts in Western Europe and Japan, in decisions to expand capital plant, to lay off surplus workers and to develop new products. At the same time, they face higher barriers to enter their rivals' home markets than foreign firms face entering US markets. US firms are at *or near the forefront in technological advances, especially in computers and in medical, aerospace, and military equipment. Their advantage has narrowed since the end of World War II. The onrush of technology largely explains the gradual development of a "two-tier labor market" in which those at the bottom lack the education and the professional/technical skills of those at the top and, more and more, fail to get comparable pay raises, health insurance coverage, and other benefits. Since 1975, practically all the gains in household income have gone to the top 20% of households. Since 1996, dividends and capital gains have grown faster than wages or any other category of after-tax income. Imported oil accounts for nearly 55% of US consumption. Crude oil prices doubled between 2001 and 2006, the year home prices peaked; higher gasoline prices ate into consumers' budgets and many individuals fell behind in their mortgage payments. Oil prices climbed another 50% between 2006 and 2008 and bank foreclosures more than doubled in the same period. Besides dampening the housing market, soaring oil prices caused a drop in the value of the dollar and deterioration in the US merchandise trade deficit, which peaked at $840 billion in 2008. The sub-prime mortgage crisis, falling home prices, investment bank failures, tight credit and the global economic downturn pushed the United States into a recession by mid-2008. GDP contracted until the third quarter of 2009, making this the deepest and longest downturn since the Great Depression. To help stabilize financial markets, in October 2008 the US Congress established a $700 billion Troubled Asset Relief Program (TARP). The government used some of these funds to purchase equity in US banks and industrial corporations, much of which had been returned to the government by early 2011. In January 2009 the US Congress passed and President Barack OBAMA signed a bill providing an additional $787 billion fiscal stimulus to be used over 10 years - two-thirds on additional spending and one-third on tax cuts - to create jobs and to help the economy recover. In 2010 and 2011, the federal budget deficit reached nearly 9% of GDP. In 2012 the federal government reduced the growth of spending and the deficit shrank to 7.6% of GDP. Wars in Iraq and Afghanistan required major shifts in national resources from civilian to military purposes and contributed to the growth of the budget deficit and public debt. Through*

7

2011, the direct costs of the wars totaled nearly $900 billion, according to US government figures. US revenues from taxes and other sources are lower, as a percentage of GDP, than those of most other countries. In March 2010, President OBAMA signed into law the Patient Protection and Affordable Care Act, a health insurance reform that was designed to extend coverage to an additional 32 million American citizens by 2016, through private health insurance for the general population and Medicaid for the impoverished. Total spending on health care - public plus private - rose from 9.0% of GDP in 1980 to 17.9% in 2010. In July 2010, the president signed the DODD-FRANK Wall Street Reform and Consumer Protection Act, a law designed to promote financial stability by protecting consumers from financial abuses, ending taxpayer bailouts of financial firms, dealing with troubled banks that were "too big to fail," and improving accountability and transparency in the financial system - in particular, by requiring certain financial derivatives to be traded in markets that are subject to government regulation and oversight. In December 2012, the Federal Reserve Board (Fed) announced plans to purchase $85 billion per month of mortgage-backed and Treasury securities in an effort to hold down long-term interest rates, and to keep short term rates near zero until unemployment drops below 6.5% or inflation rises above 2.5%. In late 2013, the Fed announced that it would begin scaling back long-term bond purchases to $75 billion per month in January 2014 and reduce them further as conditions warranted. The Fed, however, would keep short-term rates near zero so long as unemployment and inflation had not crossed the previously stated thresholds. Long-term problems include stagnation of wages for lower-income families, inadequate investment in deteriorating infrastructure, rapidly rising medical and pension costs of an aging population, energy shortages and sizable current account and budget deficits.

Table 1. 5-Year Government of USA Budget Analysis

Budget Totals	2010	2011	2012	2013	2014
Receipts	2.955t	2.627t	2.465 t	3.03t	3.34t
Outlays	3.049t	3.796t	3.649 t	$3.77 t	3.90t
Deficit(-) / Surplus(+)	-94t	-1.169t	1.184 t	-0.74t	0.56 t

t = trillion

b= billion

Table 1. 5-Year Government of USA Budget Analysis

USA's Current Economic System

The following definitions describe the USA's current economic system: **Cost:** Cost is the actual expenses incurred manufacturing goods or producing services. It includes:

1. *Manufacturing/production expenses.*
2. *Raw material costs.*
3. *Custom duties and other levies paid on imports.*
4. *Conversion costs (i.e., price of electricity, telephone service, gas, and all types of taxes and levies charged during the production process).*

Price: Price is the selling price of any commodity or service that includes the cost of a good or service plus profit (i.e., Cost + Profit = Price).

The U.S. tax system is complicated. Most people find it difficult to understand and the United States spends millions of dollars every year collecting taxes. MBBS would eliminate this complicated system and enable the United States to spend the money used to collect taxes on more useful projects. Although tax consultants would not be necessary in MBBS, they would be able to find employment in this system.

The following list of taxes shows that the U.S. tax system is quite complex:

1. Corporate Taxation: Corporate profits are taxed at a corporate tax rate and dividends paid to shareholders are taxed at a separate rate. This system is called double taxation because corporate profits paid to shareholders are taxed twice.
2. Individual Taxation: Wages and salaries, pensions, bonuses, commissions, business income, dividends, interest, capital gains, rent and royalties are taxed in the United States. Taxes are also collected for any overseas investments of a U.S. citizen. In addition, U.S. citizens and residents must pay an estate tax on inheritances.
3. International Company Taxation: U.S. companies that operate overseas must pay taxes on their profits. The laws concerning these taxes are very complex and require professional help to avoid penalties.

As described in Chapter Two, MBBS is an incentive-based system that will greatly reduce the cost of living for average people and reduce production costs for businesses. It will also produce more than enough money for the U.S. government to balance its budgets and eliminate its debts. Table 18 shows the effects MBBS will have on the United States' financial situation.

Current System (amount in trillions)	MBCS (amount in trillions)
total budget = $3.90 trillion	projected budget = $50 trillion
unemployment = 7.3%	unemployment = 0%
current debt (approx) = $35 trillion	total debt = $0.00
current VAT on retail sales = 15%	government-controlled aid = 3% (gives incentive)
Inflation @ 3 % per annum (approx)	total deflation
industrial production growth rate = 3.2%	industrial production growth rate above 100%
black money runs into trillions of dollars	no black money

Table 18. The Effects of MBBS on the United States' Financial Situation

USA's Economic System under MBBS

The following definitions describe USA's economic system under MBBS:

$. Value: $ value is a current prevailing market price. This price is not applicable to consumers and is only used to calculate the numbers of bonds needed to purchase a good or service. According to the most conservative estimates, if all the indirect taxes were abolished, production cost would be reduced by 50%. This reduced cost, which includes actual cost and profit, is the dollar value in MBBS.

> **Bond Value:** The MBBS bond value is the price of goods and services, which is twice the value of a current dollar value.
>
> **Bond:** A MBBS bond replaces all indirect taxes, custom duties, excise taxes, surcharges, and all other levies. The cheaper the bond, the less tax paid by a consumer or business.
>
> **Actual Price:** In MBBS, the actual selling price is the price a subscriber or consumer has to pay and this price depends on the cost of bonds. The cheaper the bond, the cheaper the price of the commodity or service provided by the government.
>
> **Production Cost:** In MBBS, production costs will be reduced by 50% because all direct and indirect taxes, duties, surcharges and other levies are abolished and replaced by bonds. These taxes are eliminated because the government is able to collect enough money within a few days of implementing MBBS to meets it annual budget.

In USA, 25% of the population (i.e., 75 million people) can easily spend $50,000 in the first few days to reduce their daily bills by two thirds of the previous cost. This will raise $3.75 trillion for the government, which is more than enough money to meet the government's budgetary needs. Once this money is raised, the USA would be declared a tax-free heaven, even for the foreign investor. This is one of the doors through which money will flood into Govt.'s treasury. There are five more doors through which money will flow to the government, and these will be described later in this chapter.

Philosophy of MBBS

In MBBS, a current prevailing market price is the U.S. dollar value and the other price is the bond value. The bond value is a subsidized price, with an average discount of 40% to 60% compared to the prevailing market price. The price of a bond will vary between three and five bonds per dollars, depending on the amount purchased, time of purchase, or whether they are purchased under special registration rules (up to five bonds per dollars during the whole year, depending on the type of registration).

These bonds will reduce the cost of production by at least 40%, which will reduce the cost of living. This reduced price will not be below the actual cost of a good or service and will carry at least a 10% mark-up on the cost price provided by the government.

In MBBS, it is possible for businesses to use a duty-free option. It would increase the import of technically and extremely useful high-tech industry products more than 10 times the present rate. MBBS would also increase all other types of imports because of the demand and supply factor. This duty-free environment would not hurt the government because all these imports would be carried out by the private sector, and the only role played by the government would be the removal of these unnecessary duties. As a result of the duties, the private sector imports goods from neighboring countries where these products are cheaper than they would be if American businesses tried to produce them. In MBBS, the duty on fuel would be almost nonexistent.

Tax as a Burden

In 2014, the Government of the USA collected US$ **3.34** trillion in direct and indirect taxes. This is equal to almost US$ 9,600 for every man, woman, and child in USA if social contributions were added, taxes and other revenues would amount to approximately 22% of GDP (*CIA Country Yearbook*, 2014).

1. These people are gainfully employed, and many of them are owner/managers or professionals. (Private Sector)
2. Income tax is paid by at least 48% of the population but everybody pays indirect taxes.

Given that the per capita Gross Domestic Product (GDP) of the USA is $52,800, the tax burden being carried by this small group of taxpayers is absurd.

Why The MBBS Can Work for USA

The USA's current revenue system requires indirect taxes, import duties, government duties and price controls. In addition, higher prices for controlled goods and services, as a means of collecting revenue in an economy that is performing, but with the help of very high indirect taxes is unpopular.

In order to create a successful revenue collection system in USA, it is necessary to ensure that the revenue net is spread as far as possible and there must be a general consensus among those within the net that co-operation is worthwhile.

Changing the American Mindset

MBBS provides a revenue collection system for the Government of the USA and it is based on a nationwide, dual pricing system for all goods and services and associated profits. This applies not only to Govt.-controlled goods and services, but also to goods and services provided by the private sector.

In order to enjoy lower prices, citizens prepay for a MBBS bond that is used for buying goods and services that have two prices. The revenue from the sale of these bonds goes to the government through a national monetary fund that sells bonds and collects money. In the USA, this national organization would be called the United States Monetary Fund (a private contractor) (USMF) and it would pay revenue collected from the sale of bonds directly to Govt. accounts.

MBBS is a revenue system, not a tax system. In effect, the scheme asks businesses and consumers to help the government and it encourages people to use this system by offering lower prices for goods and services. MBBS is attractive to consumers, because it appeals to people's desire to find the best deal for a good or service.

MBBS' Economic Appeal

In MBBS, there is no statutory obligation to buy bonds. The scheme relies entirely on the basic human instinct of getting the best deal. Unlike the USA's current indirect tax system, MBBS will attract people because it offers guaranteed discounts on goods and services.

The lower prices available with MBBS bonds will attract at least 25% of the population. In addition, it will attract consumers because they will pay a higher price (present price) without bonds. MBBS will eventually attract enough participants to enable the USA to eliminate its current indirect tax system. In addition, because bonds will be bought at the start of a financial year, the government will know exactly how much money it will have to fulfill its obligations during the year.

A Microeconomic Case For MBBS

MBBS will affect the micro economy of USA in the following ways:

1. All transactions involving the use of money or credit for goods and services can operate under the scheme. (Govt. Sector)
2. MBBS applies to the entire economy, including non-profit organizations.
3. MBBS will reduce household and business costs, which will increase consumer net disposable income (NDI) and business profitability.
4. MBBS will have an immediate, favorable impact on economic activity, employment and government revenues.
5. MBBS will affect the supply (e.g., imports, manufacturing, agriculture, and services) and demand (e.g., individuals, households, and business) sides of USA's economy and eliminate supply/demand curve imbalances.
6. MBBS revenues will reflect the level of economic activity in the macro economy and the system will grow proportionately with the growth of GDP.
7. MBBS incentives will reduce the need for a large bank balance and encourage more people to participate in the open economy as bond accounts will be much more profitable than interest based accounts.

MBBS in Outline

In MBBS, an American consumer would use a prepaid bond (i.e., in the form of a plastic card/voucher) when purchasing any goods or service (under Govt. Control). The consumer who uses a bond would be entitled to significant discounts on the listed sales price/cost of utility bills and other purchases.

While the scheme requires the government to discount, in some cases, its indirect tax rate/fixed pricing to people using bonds, it will increase upfront cash flows to the government. The short, medium and long-term benefits of increased and timely revenue collection will far outweigh a theoretical reduction in indirect tax rates/price controls.

MBSC will work in the favor of consumers and businesses will gain significant, preferential advantages by using bonds. Businesses will be drawn into the scheme by the simple pressure of lower prices offered by businesses that participate in MBBS.

MBBS will increase the USA's GDP and this will substantially outweigh the discount aspect of the system. In addition, MBBS will cause massive foreign currency outside the USA to migrate into MBBS-based transactions and increase Govt.'s revenue Net (see Figure 1).

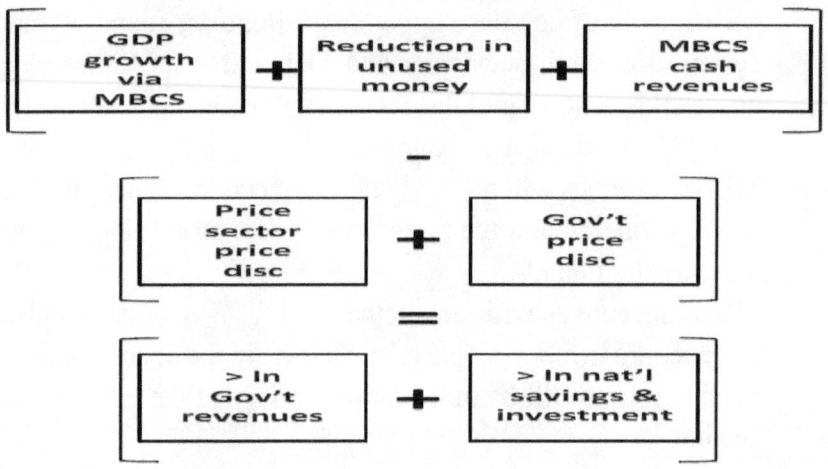

Figure 1. Economic Impact of MBBS

Why Price Controls?

The USA controls the prices of a large number of critical items:

1. Electricity.
2. Petrol, diesel and aviation fuel.

3. Telecommunication services.
4. Road taxes.
5. A large range of consumer items.
6. Registration fees, stamp duties and other government fees & licenses.
7. Court fees.
8. Fixed duties on air travel.
9. Surcharges on airline tickets.
10. Road taxes.
11. Import duties.
12. Property taxes.
13. Post office fees.
14. Fees for passports and identity cards.
15. Marriage duties.
16. Fees for private educational institutes and private and government hospitals.
17. Fees on all applications to government offices and agencies.

Govt. controls prices for a number of reasons, but it primarily controls prices in order to supplement its indirect tax revenues with profits from the sale of price controlled goods and services. In fact, it is the only way it can guarantee it will collect revenue on certain items, because a general sales tax is neither practical nor politically acceptable. MBBS would enable the Government of the USA to continue the practice of making money directly from sales and it would model the two-tiered price scheme for the private sector by offering a discount price to consumers who use MBBS bonds.

Figure 2 compares current costs for Govt.-controlled goods and services and savings under MBBS.

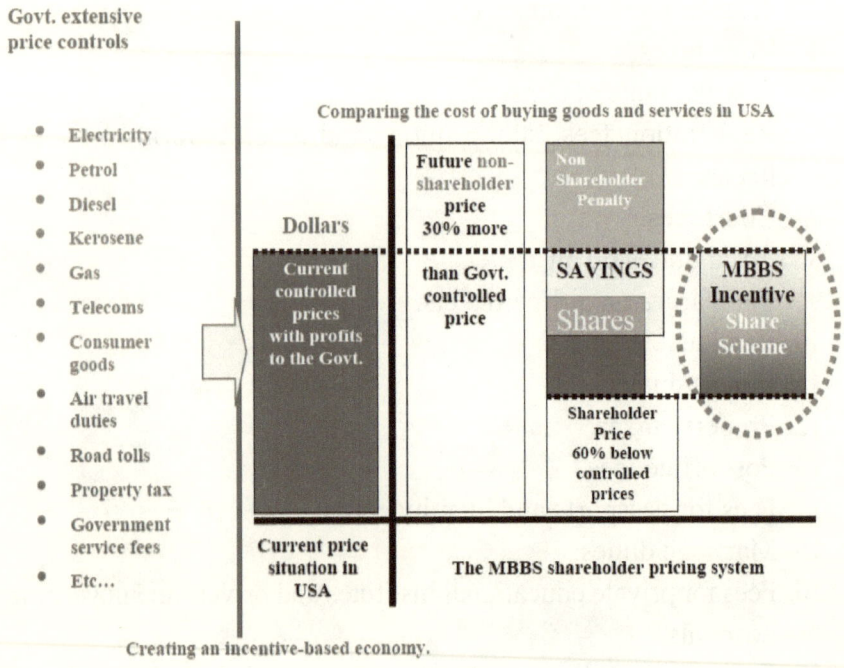

Figure 2. Comparing Costs in USA's Current System and MBBS

Figure 2. Comparing Costs in USA's Current System and MBBS

MBBS and Incentives

In the beginning, the government would offer its price-controlled items at two prices: the U.S. dollar value and bond value. The bond price is lower than the dollar price, which will become an artificial price and it offers a considerable advantage over the artificial price in real cash terms. In order to enjoy the lower price, consumers would pay twice as many bonds as dollars for the same good or service. This appears to be a win-win situation for consumers if bonds are bought at a rate below face value (e.g., five bonds per dollar or even three or four bonds per dollar). Consumers would save at least 20%, even if the rate was three bonds per U.S. dollar. However, in the open market, the rate of bonds per dollar would always be above three bonds per dollar. (see Figure 3).

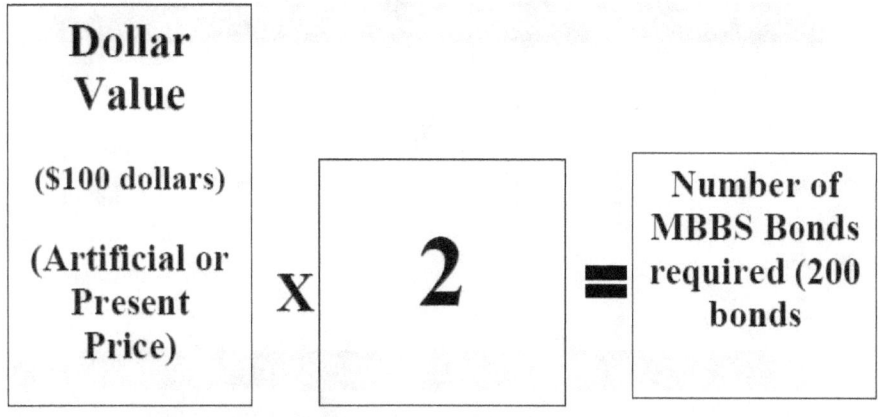

Figure 3. Current Price System's Relationship to MBBS

MBBS Prices

In MBBS, there are two stated prices and one final price (see Figure 4):

1. The first stated price is the artificial price, called dollar value (stated on label/list). This price is used only to calculate the number of MBBS bonds required and will be the prevailing market price.
2. The second price is the with-bond price, called bond value (stated on label/list). This price is 40% to 60% lower than current prices and will (depending on the bond rate per dollar at the time) show how many bonds are needed for the purchase.
3. The third and final price is the actual price in dollars. This is the price in dollars actually paid by the consumer once the number of bonds is calculated.

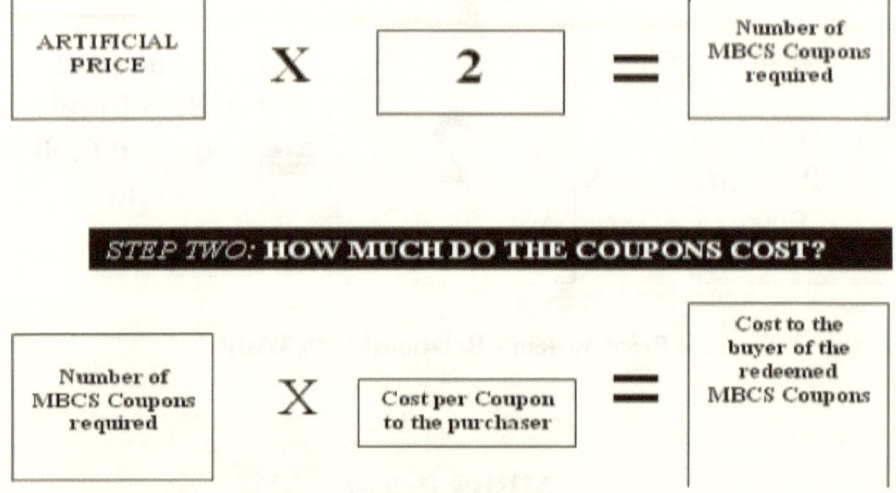

Coupons /Bonds Figure 4. Calculating Actual Price

Calculating the Cost of Bonds

It is quite easy to calculate the cost of MBBS bonds: More bonds equal lower costs, and earlier bond purchases in a financial year equals more benefits. The incentive to participate in MBBS is lower prices for goods and services. In addition consumers are rewarded for buying more bonds early in a financial year. Table 2 shows the benefits of buying bonds in bulk: For example, a consumer could spend from 0.33 dollar to 0.20 dollar per bond, depending on the time of year the bonds are purchased.

Month		Official Bond Cost	Open Market Rate
1	January	100% of special concession*	
2	February	70% of special concession*	
3	March	50% of special concession*	
4	April		3 to 5 per dollar depending upon the availability of number of bonds
5	May		
6	June	Bonds available on the market	
7	July	at the rates set out in	
8	August	Official tables	
9	September		
10	October	(Lowest exchange rate)	
11	November		
12	December		

*During the first financial quarter of each year, MBCS would operate under a special concession arrangement to encourage the maximum upfront purchase of bonds. The concession enables any person, household, or business to buy at a rate of five bonds per U.S. dollar in the first month, which is the maximum amount, and will keep on decreasing over time.

Table 2. Benefits of Buying Bonds in Bulk

The Rationale for a Sliding Scale for Bond Costs

The financial objective of MBBS is to deliver substantial upfront revenues (i.e., liquidity) to Govt. and improve its solvency (e.g., balanced budgets). MBBS uses a sliding scale to encourage people to buy large quantities of bonds early in a financial year. There are four reasons to use a sliding scale for bond costs:

1. A sliding scale encourages people to buy large quantities of bonds in the first month of a financial year.
2. It encourages the largest possible sales in single transactions.
3. It encourages non-bank deposits to buy bonds.
4. It rewards the good customers.

The sliding scale has several implications for consumers:

1. Consumers with large cash deposits, whether in or out of the official economy, will be encouraged to buy large quantities of bonds. The bonds will have significant value to high, middle and low-income households because MBBS bonds will be used to purchase all goods and services, from luxuries to necessities.
2. Bonds are bearer entitled and the holder of a bond will enjoy its benefits. Therefore, bonds can be traded on the open market and sold at a profit.
3. Buyers of bonds can trade in futures by taking options from traders on their future requirements at mutually agreed rates. This is particularly important because bonds will be available through official channels at their best rates only during the early part of a financial year; however, consumers who can buy more than $250,000 worth of bonds would be able to obtain a rate of 5 bonds per dollar throughout the year.
4. The costs of living and production will be reduced and create consumer demand, savings, and increased profit.

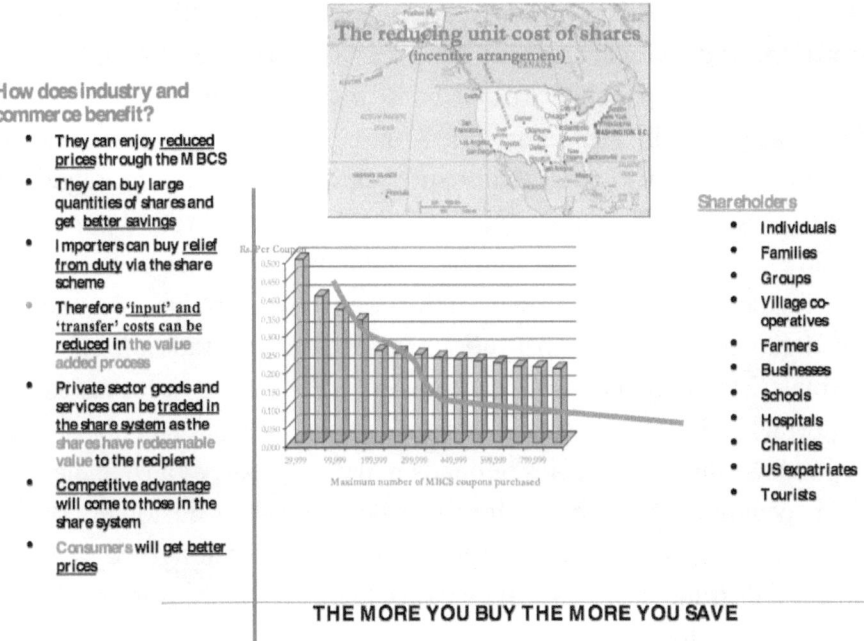

How does industry and commerce benefit?

- They can enjoy reduced prices through the MBCS
- They can buy large quantities of shares and get better savings
- Importers can buy relief from duty via the share scheme
- Therefore 'input' and 'transfer' costs can be reduced in the value added process
- Private sector goods and services can be traded in the share system as the shares have redeemable value to the recipient
- Competitive advantage will come to those in the share system
- Consumers will get better prices

Shareholders

- Individuals
- Families
- Groups
- Village co-operatives
- Farmers
- Businesses
- Schools
- Hospitals
- Charities
- US expatriates
- Tourists

THE MORE YOU BUY THE MORE YOU SAVE

Creating an incentive-based economy acceptable to Human nature.

Figure 5. Sliding Scale for Bond Costs

Reasons for Purchasing MBBS Bonds

There are three reasons why a consumer would want to purchase MBBS bonds:

1. Bond-based transactions are less expensive than dollar-based transactions.
2. Bonds purchased at the beginning of a financial year are less expensive than bonds purchased later in the year.
3. The cheaper the bonds, the cheaper the price of the goods and services bought using bonds.

The best deals (i.e., rates for bonds) will come through official channels during the first financial quarter. This will attract substantial revenues ahead of purchasing requirements, and it will be a win-win situation for the Government of USA and it's consumers.

The more expensive official bond market in the remainder of a financial year will encourage open market trading among businesses and individuals who trade bond surpluses for shortfalls at negotiated prices. This market is important because it creates a broad-based value for an exchange market that is independent of Govt. price controls. This will further support the growth of the bond system in the open market.

Banks and financial institutions will be able to trade through their normal distribution channels and provide MBBS bond accounts as well as normal U.S. dollar cash and deposit accounts. Banks will also be able to purchase larger quantities of bonds in the early part of a financial year on a speculative basis and offer these bonds to their customers during the year. Banks can top up customer bond accounts at agreed rates and times. This trade in bonds will be a very lucrative business for banks and a valuable customer service.

Approximately 80% of the USA's population pays for the basics of modern living, such as telephones, gas, water, electricity and so forth. MBBS will offer cheaper actual prices on the consumption of these important everyday basics. The following steps show how the price for a basic commodity is calculated using MBBS:

1. When calculating the bill for a commodity, the vendor uses present prevailing tariff charges.
2. When the bill is paid, bonds will replace dollars and the savings will depend on the rate of bonds when they were purchased. Utility bills will calculate/show the number of bonds required by the user, so there will be no confusion or need for the consumer to do the calculating.
3. The bond value price of the utility will be much lower than the dollar value price.

Figures 6, 7, and 8 show how MBBS affects the price of electricity for large, medium, and small consumers. Table 3 shows the cost of petrol under MBBS.

USA Electricity Billing Authority (Reg. Under MBCS)		Costs in $	Bonds
	Calculations		
1	Units last reading	12500	
2	Units this reading	13500	
3	Units consumed*	1000	
4	$. Value Price	suppose	1000
5	Bond Value Price		2000
6	Bonds required		2000

	Bonds
Total MBCS bonds to pay bill	2000

*Existing electricity tariff cost to consumer (2014) $100

How much does the electricity really cost me if?	
I.e. How much benefit do I get from the bonds?	
1	How many MBCS bonds do I need?	2000
2	How much do they cost me in $ @ 3 per table?	666.66
3	And what is the Total $ cost of my bill?	666.66
4	* And savings from the existing tariff above?	444.44

How much does the electricity really cost me if?	
I.e. How much benefit do I get from the bonds?	
1	How many MBCS bonds do I need?	2000
2	How much do they cost me in $ @ 4 per table?	500
3	And what is the Total dollar cost of my bill?	500
4	* And savings from the existing tariff above?	500

How much does the electricity really cost me?	
I.e. How much benefit do I get from the bonds?	
1	How many MBCS bonds do I need?	2000
2	How much do they cost me in $ @ 5 per table?	400
3	And what is the total dollar cost of my bill?	400
4	* And the savings from the existing tariff above?	600

MBCS bond table	
1-29,999	0.500
30,000-59,999	0.400
60,000-99,999	0.364
100,000-149,999	0.333
150,000-199,000	0.250
200,000-249,999	0.244
250,000-299,999	0.238
300,000-349,999	0.233
350,000-399,999	0.227
400,000-449,999	0.222
450,000-499,999	0.217
500,000 and above	0.200

Figure 6. Electric Bill for Large Consumers in MBBS

USA Electricity Billing Authority (Reg. Under MBCS)		Costs in $	Bonds
	Calculations		
1	Units last reading	2500	
2	Units this reading	2600	
3	Units consumed*	100	
4	Artificial price		100
5	Total subsidized price			200
6	Bonds required			200

	Bonds
Total MBCS bonds to pay bill	200

*Existing electricity tariff cost to consumer (2014) $100

How much does the electricity really cost me if?	
I.e. How much benefit do I get from the bonds?	
1	How many MBCS bonds do I need?	200
2	How much do they cost me in $ @ 3 per table?	66
3	And what is the Total $ cost of my bill?	66
4	* And savings from the existing tariff above?	33

MBCS bond table	
1-29,999	0.500
30,000-59,999	0.400
60,000-99,999	0.364
100,000-149,999	0.333
150,000-199,000	0.250
200,000-249,999	0.244
250,000-299,999	0.238
300,000-349,999	0.233
350,000-399,999	0.227
400,000-449,999	0.222
450,000-499,999	0.217
500,000 and above	0.20

How much does the electricity really cost me if?	
I.e. How much benefit do I get from the bonds?	
1	How many MBCS bonds do I need?	200
2	How much do they cost me in $ @ 4 per table?	50
3	And what is the Total $ cost of my bill?	50
4	* And savings from the existing tariff above?	50

How much does the electricity really cost me?	
I.e. How much benefit do I get from the bonds?	
1	How many MBCS bonds do I need?	200
2	How much do they cost me in $ @ 5 per table?	40
3	And what is the total $ cost of my bill?	40
4	* And the savings from the existing tariff above?	60

Figure 7. Electric Bill for Medium Consumers in MBBS

			$ Value Price (Current Price) =		
			$ Value Price (Current Price) =	$ 2.20	220 dollars
			Bond Value Price =	4.4 Bonds	440 Bonds
Typical Purchaser	Quantity (Gallons)	$ Value Price ($)	Bond Value Price (Bonds)		
				3	4	5
	1	2.20	4.4	1.46	1.10	0.88
	10	22.00	44	14.66	11.00	8.80
	20	44.00	88	29.33	22.00	17.60
	40	88.00	176	58.66	44.00	35.20
	60	132.00	264	88.00	66.00	52.80
	80	176.00	352	117.33	88.00	70.40
	100	220.00	440	146.66	110.00	88.00
	200	440.00	880	293.33	220.00	176.00
	300	660.00	1320	440.00	330.00	264.00
	400	880.00	1760	586.66	440.00	352.00

Table 3. Suppose Cost of Petrol in MBBS for 100 gallons

In MBBS, all government-controlled prices (e.g., government fees, post office fees, hospital fees, railway tickets, and airline tickets) will be available by paying twice the number of bonds as the prevailing price (see 5 for some examples).

Bonds Required 400	Net Price ($)	Savings ($)	Savings%
Cost of 400 Bonds @ 3	133	77	33.33
Cost of 400 Bonds @ 4	100	100	50
Cost of 400 Bonds @ 5	80	120	60

Note: Airline tickets (with duties and taxes) under present system cost $200. Under MBCS, a ticket can be purchased using double the amount in bonds. Number of bonds required is 200 * 2 = 400.

Table 5. Example of an Airline Ticket $200

All duties will disappear after the system is implemented in total and private businesses will opt for government as a sleeping partner contributing 80% of liquidity with zero interest but sharing profit and loss in all these businesses in the ratio of 40 to 60% see the detail under interest free banking.

The Household Budget and MBBS

MBBS will deliver real benefits to the basic economic units of consumption to the household and the individual. MBBS enables consumers who plan their expenses to maximize their savings through the calculated use of the marginal bond cost mechanism. In essence, MBBS encourages purchases in bulk at the start of a financial year. Householders and individuals who are able to assess their needs for the period ahead will be able to accurately decide how many bonds to purchase.

The bond needs of households fall into four basic categories:

1. *Basic consumption needs required to sustain living,*
2. *Luxury items that bring comfort over and above basic needs,*
3. *Contingencies that deal with the unexpected in life, and*
4. *Speculation that covers the desire to profit from the investment of surplus funds.*

MBBS bonds apply to all these situations, and individuals can use the purchase of bonds to leverage greater value for their money and use the savings to invest.

MBBS and the Concept of Marginal Utility

The concept of utility and its relationship to the quantity of any item or service purchased is a cornerstone of microeconomics. Utility is the benefit derived by the buyer from a purchase, and beyond a certain point, the buyer loses the benefit of quantity. This is called marginal utility and it drives the price people are willing to pay for a good or service. For example, the utility of a glass of water to a man dying of thirst in the desert is very high. The marginal utility of the next glass of water is also very high. The same cannot be said of a man with ample access to free water. The same concept applies to the MBBS bond. It is also different because money and MBBS bonds do not satisfy needs directly. They are used to exchange for goods and services that have intrinsic value/utility. However, the MBBS bond has high utility, because it can be used for exchange at value. MBBS bonds would be purchased to cover a number of useful purposes, and the utility of bonds can be expressed in savings and speculation. All households and businesses would purchase MBBS bonds for four basic purposes, depending on means and disposition:

1. They would buy bonds to save money on planned necessities and luxuries.
2. To provide for unplanned expenditures in the future.
3. To provide room for discretionary expenditures.
4. To speculate on the price of MBBS bonds using volume purchases or accumulation.

Table 7 shows how a consumer can use MBBS bonds.

Generic Bond Use	Application	Utility or Value	Utility Factor by Income Group		
			High	Medium	Low
Speculative	Store surplus	MBCS bond purchasers speculate by accumulating surplus bonds or by buying large discounted quantities to sell at profit	Bond utility is high if the prosperity / attractiveness to speculation is high	Bond utility is high if the prosperity / attractiveness to speculation is high	Bond utility is high if the prosperity / attractiveness to speculation is high
	Buy to sell				
	Buy to save				
	Buy to hoard				
	Forward selling				
	Forward buying				
Contingencies	Increased basics	Purchasing more MBCS bonds than planned needs enables discretionary choice in the future. This is of high value when income exceeds the planned expenditure on basics and a few luxuries	High-income consumers will understand the benefit of bond purchases beyond planned essentials and luxuries	Bond utility becoming marginal beyond contingencies for increased basics and a few more luxuries	Bond utility is marginal at best
	More luxuries				
	Marriages, births				
	Gifts				
	Travel				
	Rainy days				
	Poor estimating				
Luxuries	Car	The line between luxuries & basic is very difficult to draw. However, the utility of these items is high for all income groups and is the utility of the MBCS bonds with which to purchase them	Considered as basic needs by many high income groups and. Therefore, high utility for bonds	Utility varies by type of goods or service but bond purchase utility is still high	Bond utility is high once basics are met
	TV				
	VCR				
	White goods				
	Computers				
	Holidays				
Basic Consumption Needs	Electricity	High utility for all basic needs; therefore. bonds are essential			
	Water				
	Food				
	Petrol				
	Clothing				
	Gas				

Table 7. Consumer's Use of MBBS Bonds

It should also be kept in mind that as the net disposable income of a household increases so does their view of utility. Luxuries become essentials. In other words, as GDP grows, consumers will demand more MBBS bonds. The cost reductions created by MBBS will enhance savings and investment.

Why MBBS Bonds Help Businesses

The MBBS bond system can help all businesses. In order to participate in MBBS, businesses must register with the USMF. All businesses that participate in MBBS are divided into three simple categories, which does away with the myriad of registrations currently in place.

Category One Business

A Category One business passes its goods and services on to an end user (i.e., consumers) and it can register at the start of the year for the upfront sum of $10,000 or multiple of $10,000. This fee entitles the business to 20,000 bonds at five bonds per dollar, provided the business can show that it has collected 10000 bonds. These bonds could be purchased on the open market or from a customer. The second option is much more business oriented and therefore, the business would collect more bonds and charge a lower cash price to increase its number of customers. These bonds would be surrendered to the USMF in exchange of new bonds without cost. This would eliminate the repeated use of the same bonds by other people or businesses because there would be a record of the issue date. The collection of bonds depends on the registration fee. The more the registration fee, the more the bonds a business can purchase at the rate of 5 bonds per dollar. The registration fee would entitle a business to purchase additional bonds for $4,000 (i.e. 20,000/500). This in itself is a cash rebate and the value depends on the open market exchange rate or the official rate, whichever is better. Table 8 shows the sliding scale of benefits because there is no actual cash limit to the registration fee, and it is a very cost-effective way for businesses to purchase 20,000 or more MBBS bonds at the rate 5 per dollar through out the year for a minimum registration of $10,000. The incentive keeps on increasing with higher amount of registration as shown below in table no 8.

Business Registration Table							
With Registration Fee Purchase				Normal Purchase			
Reg. Fee $	Bonds Collection Entitlement	Entitlement to No. of Bonds to Purchase @ 5 per dollar	Amount $	Amount $	Rate of Bond	No. of Bond	
10,000	1,0000	2,0000	4,000	10,000	2	2,000,000	
30,000	3,0000	7,5000	15,000	30,000	2.5	7,500,000	
60,000	6,0000	16,5000	33,000	60,000	2.75	16,500,000	
100,000	10,0000	300000	60,000	100,000	3	30,000,000	
150,000	150000	600000	120,000	150,000	4	60,000,000	
200,000	200000	820000	164,000	200,000	4.1	82,000,000	
250,000	250000	100,000	210,000	250,000	4.2	105,000,000	
300,000	30,0000	129,0000	258,000	300,000	4.3	129,000,000	
400,000	40,0000	176,0000	352,000	400,000	4.4	176,000,000	
450,000	45,0000	202,500,00	405,000	450,000	4.5	202,500,000	
500,000	50,0000	230,00000	460,000	500,000	4.6	230,000,000	
550,000	55,0000	258,50000	470,000	550,000	4.7	258,500,000	
600,000	60,0000	288,00000	576,000	600,000	4.8	288,000,000	
700,000	70,0000	343,00000	686,000	700,000	4.9	343,000,000	
800,000	80,0000	400,00000	800,000	800,000	5	400,000,000	
And above	And above	And above	And above	And above		And above	

Note: These are approximate but incentive based ratios and can be changed according to country's requirement.

Table 8. Registration Fees for Businesses

Category Two Business

A Category Two business does not trade up the value chain in bonds, but it can still purchase MBBS bonds for it's ordinary expenses/ purchases. This type of business can register with the USMF for $10,000 or multiples of $10,000. This fee would entitle the business to register for 20,000 bonds per month or multiples of 20,000 bonds at a special rate of five bonds per dollar throughout the year.

Category Three Business

A Category Three business may elect to establish a special relationship with the USMF by agreeing to sell its entire output to USMF for pre-agreed market prices plus 5% in cash or 15% in bonds. In addition, it would be entitled to import all its capital and other needs into the USA, duty free, at a value equal to what it sells to the USMF if the business opts for duty free option and doesn't want bonds.

The combined effect of a supply of bonds up to 15% of the value generated by production and the reduction of costs through the removal of duty on imported items would improve operating margins. Input costs would be substantially reduced, and output prices would stabilize. In addition, these businesses can earn 5 bonds per dollar if the duty free option is not taken, which would further decrease the costs of inputs as these businesses will not have to spend billions upfront (see the Gold Mine section).

The Impact of Participating in MBBS

In MBBS, all three categories of businesses would experience a reduction in the basic costs of doing business. Transforming activity into value for most businesses involves purchasing the following:

1. Capital equipment.
2. Materials and finished items.
3. Energy.

Each of these items is available to a business under the MBBS scheme. Capital equipment, materials, and finished goods can be purchased through the USMF by surrendering plus 5% in cash or 15% in bonds. Imported goods are also offered on the same basis, with all tariffs and duties removed. If this system is strung along the entire chain of business value-added activity, the impact on costs, prices, and margin will be significant.

In MBBS, businesses would have the opportunity to accept cash and bonds at the point of sale. Their customers and competitors may choose for them because it will be difficult to sell goods and services outside MBBS. Price competition will be too intense. Businesses will also experience lower operating costs if they participate in MBBS. Travel, telephone calls, petrol, registration fees, stationary, computers, and so forth would be available in MBBS, and the reduced prices available using bonds would have a significant, positive impact on expenses and overheads.

Savings for Manufacturers in MBBS

Table 10 shows the savings available to a Category One business. This Table describes manufacturing costs based on buying bonds or applying for the duty-free option. The Category 3 registration of $50,000 would entitle a business to sell merchandise at a maximum of 10 times the registration fee per month or $500,000 worth of goods through the USMF in one installment or in, at the most, 12 installments, with each transaction not less than $0.5 million. This would reduce the work of USMF to a great extent.

Manufacturers who sell their products through the USMF would have to deposit 5% in cash or 15% in bonds of the amount of product sold to USMF. This would entitle a producer to purchase bonds at the rate of five bonds per dollar or obtain duty-free imports, depending on the amount sold. The value of the 15% in bonds would be three dollars (if the rate is five bonds per dollar) per $100. Consumers would happily pay 15% in bonds because the goods are cheaper as a result of the 50% reduction in production costs. Producers would declare 100% or more of their end products because they want to get back their registration fees by selling extra bonds at the open-market rate, duty-free goods, or options to other buyers.

Gold Mine

MBBS will be a gold mine for the Government of the USA, because it would receive at least three percent of the profit from everything produced or sold in the market. The gold from this mine would flow to Govt. in the following way:

A Category 3 business cannot invest the billions of dollars needed to buy cheap bonds at the beginning of a financial year, so they would sell their products through the USMF. This arrangement would entitle the business to buy cheap bonds or duty-free goods equal to the amount of merchandise sold, and the quota would be 10 times the amount of the registration fee. A registration fee of $50,000 would entitle a business to sell $6 million worth of goods through the USMF per year, but it would have to surrender 15% of the amount sold in bonds to the USMF at the time of sale. These bonds would be returned to Govt., and in return, Govt. would allow the business to purchase five bonds per dollar or obtain duty-free goods and services throughout the year equal to the amount sold through the USMF. These bonds would be resold by Govt., which would keep this profit.

Figure 9 illustrates this gold mine.

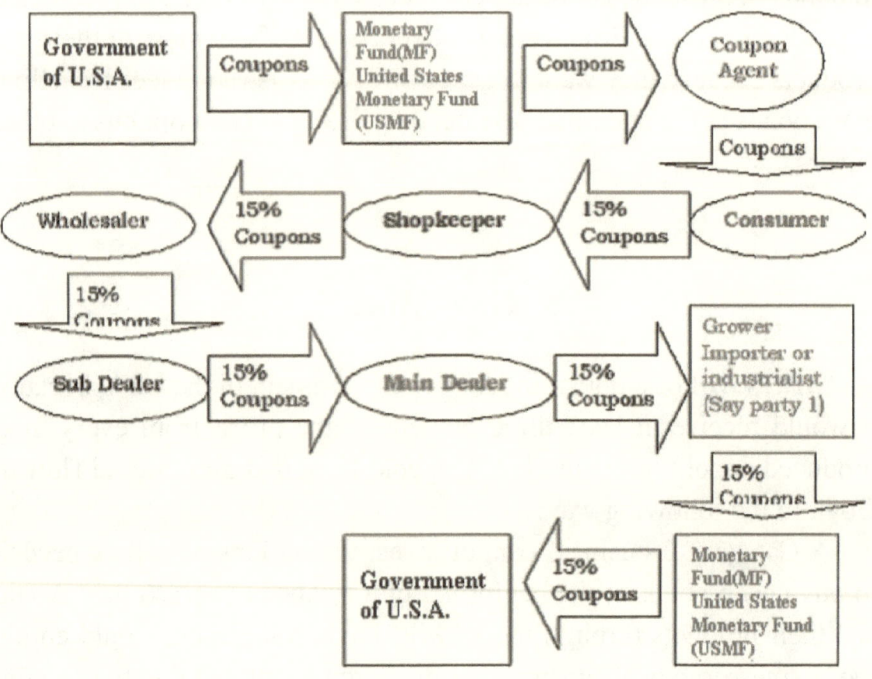

The Retailer and MBBS

The benefits of MBBS will cascade down to independent retailers, because the use of bonds and lower prices for manufactured goods, will enable retailers to offer consumers lower prices. Retailers will receive special rates for bonds collected from sales and reduce their costs when purchasing stock. Retailers will have the opportunity to discount prices in MBBS and accept MBBS bonds in return for discounted with-bond prices.

The method for calculating retail prices will be different from the method used to determine the prices of Govt.-price-controlled goods and services. The actual cost to a retailer is cash plus the cost of the 15% in bonds. This cost may vary, because the actual price paid for bonds is not fixed.

Bonds collected by a retailer can be traded and used for discounting business-related expenses. Therefore, they represent value to a business. In addition, under the rules of MBBS, the collection of bonds by registered businesses entitles these businesses to buy two to no upper limit (depends on the registration fee) of MBBS bonds at the rate of 5 bonds per U.S. dollar. Bonds have tangible value for exchange and trading purposes, and therefore, businesses will be able to account for bonds in their financial results.

A retailer of a shirt, for example, will calculate price in MBBS based on a number of business considerations:

1. Desired operating profit.
2. The cost of the shirt.
3. Desire for MBBS bonds.
4. The competitive policy of rivals.

Retailers of shirts, or any other good or service, are unlikely to ignore MBBS because the price of a shirt outside MBBS makes the shirt business unprofitable. Table 11 shows not only the input cost of a shirt, but also the possible sales price if the vendor decides to sell the shirt for cash and bonds, which is much less than the present price.

Business Operations and MBBS

At the end of each year, businesses draw up accounts that demonstrate their business performance in financial terms. In MBBS, accounting for operations will also show how many MBBS bonds were collected and an assessment of their net worth.

The key question is how does a retailer optimize profits and minimize risk in MBBS. After all, retailers are asked to accept less value prima facie for their goods in MBBS than in the previous system. This question is at the core of MBBS because it applies equally to small, medium, and large businesses, as it does to the Government of USA and its agencies.

A rational business has the following objectives:

1. Maximize profits and minimize losses.
2. Maintain a positive cash flow (cash in – cash out = > 0).
3. Recover at least all direct and indirect operating costs.
4. Minimize risk.
5. Invest cash surpluses in the business.

To achieve these objectives in MBBS, a business will have to:

1. Operate at a level of discount that recovers at least the cash cost of the items for sale, and in this regard, the business can operate separate discount arrangements when the cash costs as a percentage of selling price differ.
2. Use MBBS to buy wholesale goods and services manufactured in the USA and outside under tax-free and discount import arrangements. This would reduce the cash cost to a business and offer greater scope for deciding discount levels.
3. Use MBBS bonds to discount all cost inputs, including electricity, travel, stationary, equipment, and so forth.
4. Use discretion when using preferential bonds (i.e., take account of cash positions and the risk in bond markets).
5. Use additional bond facilities to promote growth in business activities/operations.
6. Accumulate bonds, as a hedge against future needs only if cheaper sources of bonds do not exist. Table 12 shows a number of operating scenarios. This Table reveals that business operations can be attractive if additional bond entitlements are exercised. A business would use these entitlements for future trading and growth. A business' choice of the discount scenario and the related returns/risks is a business judgement that tests the business' appetite for risk, returns, and growth.

Table 12 forecasts and analyzes the impact of MBBS on the operations of a small retail business over the course of a business year. It contains the basic elements of a profit and loss projection together with the number of bonds collected during the normal course of business under a number of discount scenarios. A risk analysis is also undertaken below the bottom line to determine the impact on profit of holding large amounts of bonds.

Retailer Bottom Line Performance Registered MBBS Business					
	Discount Scheme Chosen				
	40	30	20	10	Old System
Cash Revenues					
MBBS cash sales	6,000,000	7,000,000	8,000,000	9,000,000	10,000,000
Cost of sales	6,000,000	6,000,000	6,000,000	6,000,000	6,000,000
Overhead cost	200,000	2,000,000	2,000,000	2,000,000	2,000,000
Direct cost discounted for bonds @ 15%	5,700,000	5,700,000	5,700,000	5,700,000	
Overheads reduced by 20% MBBS effect	1,600,000	1,600,000	1,600,000	1,600,000	
Cost of bonds used @ 5	283,333	283,333	283,333	283,333	
Adjusted cost of sales	7,583,333	7,583,333	7,583,333	7,583,333	
Operating cash profit	(1,583,333)	(583,333)	416,667	1,416,667	2,000,000
Finance charges +/-	(158,333)	(58,333)	41,667	141,667	200,000
Net profit	(1,741,666)	(641,666)	458,334	1,558,334	2,200,000
Bonds					
Bonds collected	8,000,000	6,000,000	4,000,000	2,000,000	
Minimum bond value @ 5	1,333,333	1,000,000	666,667	333,333	
Maximum bond value @ 2.5	3,200,000	2,400,000	1,600,000	800,000	
Median value	2,266,667	1,700,000	1,133,333	566,667	
Cash & bond profit best case	1,458,334	1,758,334	2,058,334	2,358,334	
Cash & bond profit worst case	(408,333)	358,334	1,125,000	1,891,667	
Cash & bond profit median case	525,000	1,058,334	1,591,667	2,125,000	
Optional MBBS Scheme					
Additional Bond					
Additional bond entitlement	24,000,000	18,000,000	12,000,000	6,000,000	
Cost of buying additional bond	4,000,000	3,000,000	2,000,000	1,000,000	
Total cash cost of bond	4,000,000	3,000,000	2,000,000	1,000,000	
Total Bond Held					
Total collected & purchased	32,000,000	24,000,000	16,000,000	8,000,000	
Bond used by business above the line	1,700,000	1,700,000	1,700,000	1,700,000	
Balance of c bonds	30,300,000	22,300,000	14,300,000	6,300,000	
Bond Value					
Value of bond held @ 2.5	12,120,000	8,920,000	5,720,000	2,520,000	
Value of bond held @5	5,050,000	3,716,667	2,383,333	1,050,000	
Median value	8,585,000	6,318,333	4,051,667	1,785,000	
Risk Analysis					
Best outcome	6,536,667	5,336,667	4,136,667	2,936,667	2,200,000
Worst outcome	(533,333)	133,333	800,000	1,466,667	2,200,000
Median outcome	3,001,667	2,735,000	2,468,334	2,201,667	2,200,000
Best outcome of capital employed %	56.43	50.43	43.17	34.21	
Worst outcome of capital employed %	(4.60)	1.26	8.35	17.09	27.50
Median	25.92	25.85	25.76	25.65	
Risk Analysis	High	Low/Medium	Low	No Risk	High Risk

A business must decide business strategies for upcoming years (e.g., pricing policy). In MBBS, a business would have to decide how much risk it is willing to assume in the form of the number of bonds held/

traded. Table 12 shows 40%, 30%, 20% and 10% discount models, with the balance up to the with-bond sales price.

In the 40% discount scheme, which means a business accepts 40% of the with bond price in MBBS bonds, a business could double its margin, depending on bond rates. It could also lose money if the rate for MBBS bonds falls below five bonds per U.S. dollar. A business' margin drops with the drop of bonds accepted, but so does its risk. A rational businessman would opt for a discount that does not cost money, regardless of the MBBS bond rate. Risk is reduced considerably after 20%, and margins remain very healthy.

In MBBS, a business would sell many shirt products with different profit margins, which are the critical driver of risk to the enterprise. When margins improve under the scheme, there is more latitude for discounting. This avoids problems associated with cash flow and negative margins. Therefore, a business may choose not to plan its discount across the board, but decide on a generic pricing policy of different discounts on different brands and lines, taking account of its cash margin, volume of sales and the pricing strategies of competitors. In the final analysis, a business would keep an eye on competitors' MBBS pricing policies and how attractive this is to buyers of shirts. This model can be applied to all retail businesses or businesses selling to an end user. It shows how flexible and profitable MBBS can be for well-run businesses.

Imports and Foreign Exchange Transactions Imports

The importation of foreign currency and goods is another source of value at the microeconomic level in the USA. There are two reasons why these imports are important: First, these imports represent significant value in the country, and second, these imports are the single greatest source of previously black money in the USA.

A Macroeconomic Case For MBBS

MBBS would generate much more revenue for the Government of the USA than the present revenue system. In addition, MBBS would resolve the systemic crisis that is causing the USA's entire economy to seriously under perform.

The macroeconomic impact of MBBS focuses on a number of economic drivers that result in the output of the economy expressed as Gross Domestic Product (GDP). The impact of MBBS at a macro level focuses on the economic system in the USA that supports GDP. This is the way that capital and finance, trade and manufacturing, agriculture and services, tax policy and tax systems, human resources (including employment), national infrastructure, interest rates, imports and exports, and so forth operate together to produce wealth.

What is wrong with the Current Economic System in the USA?

The indirect tax system causes the largest problem for the USA's economy. This system may threaten to sink the ship of state in an ocean of debt in the near future. In addition, this malfunctioning system has a negative effect on all other systems. For example stable exchange rates, investment in people and industry, low-cost financing and so forth are not possible, because the direct and indirect tax system is the main obstacle. This reinforces economic failure, and beyond a certain point, it can cause the economy to collapse.

The failure of Govt. to collect enough revenue through taxation is the result of a failed tax system and it has forced the government to use their own resources in large amounts of money in order to finance regular government deficits. The vast majority of this expense is the barrowed money with interest. Again, when a major part of an economic system starts to fail, then the entire system's performance is in jeopardy.

Figure 10 illustrates the fragile state of USA's economic system and why it is under performing. As with all macroeconomics, it is a complex system that requires skills at the highest level to manage. This is usually the job of government. However, at the grassroots level of any economic system is the investor: the person, corporate body, group of investors, institutions, pension funds, and so forth who decide to defer expenditure/dividends in favor of investment. In the USA, the investor is faced with obstacles if he/she wishes to create wealth through investment because of low returns, high risks, import duties, high commodity prices and most significant, high direct and indirect taxes. No economy in this basic condition can hope to develop long-term strength and growth.

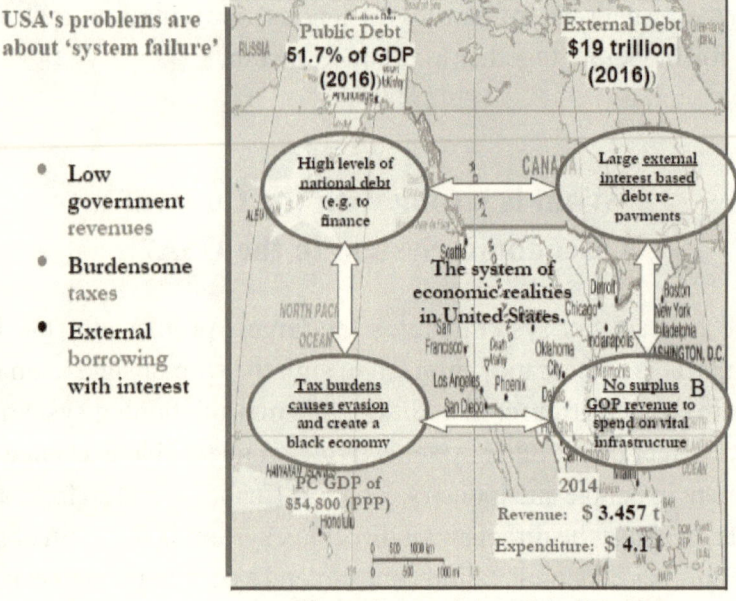

What are the economic issues facing United States

Figure 10. Fragile State of USA's Economy

The Way Out of the Crisis

In times of crisis, it is sometimes difficult to see the issues clearly because crisis management shortens and narrows people's vision. In the case of the USA and other developed countries, it is difficult to look beyond the current system and the way taxes are collected. However, if a solution is to be found, then it must be outside the current tax system. As stated elsewhere and as is generally accepted among experts and the general public, USA's current tax system does not work and more important, is unlikely to meet future needs.

MBBS would meet not only the short-term needs of the USA, it would also provide a system that creates wealth and prosperity for a large proportion of the USA's population. In short, MBBS would produce four first-order results immediately:

1. Collect more than $3 trillion in first 30 days of operation and at least 100 times more by the end of fiscal year.
2. Enable Govt. to achieve short-, medium-, and long-term solvency (i.e., USA would be able to balance its budget, avoid external debt, and invest in the country's future).

Figure 11 illustrates how MBBS would improve USA's economy.

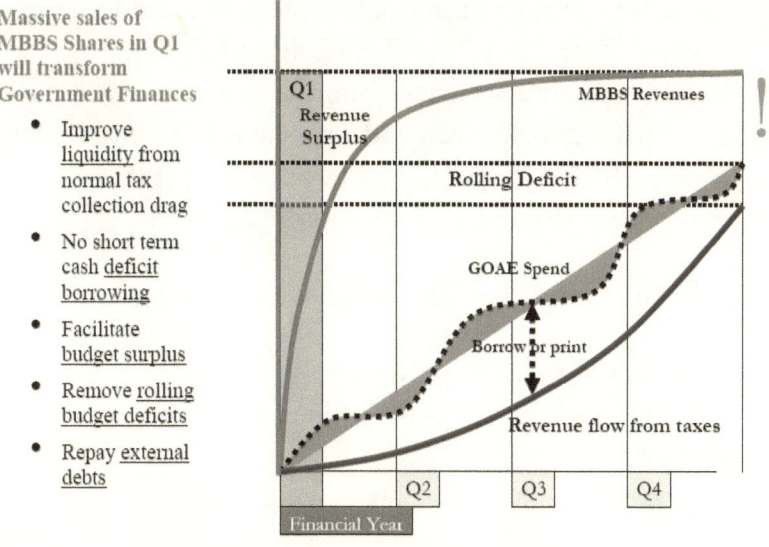

Creating an incentive based economy

Figure 11. How MBBS would improve USA's Economy

MBBS would produce a properly functioning economic system characterized

1. Balanced budgets.
2. Improved confidence in the system.
3. Investment in the infrastructure.
4. Continuous economic growth.

How MBBS Produces a Properly Functioning Economic System

MBBS works on the principle that:

1. The Government of the USA will discount its current prices for controlled goods and services in order to obtain upfront funds and lower input costs, which will promote the growth of GDP.
2. MBBS will transfer value from imports and supplies of goods and services to manufacturing units to the core added-value activities in agriculture, manufacturing, retail, and services;
3. MBBS will attract money from the black money, because the new MBBS pricing levels will compete with it for customers, and because MBBS provides for speculation, and the extra money will be used to purchase bonds for trade.

MBBS will produce four first-orders (i.e., short-term) results:

1. Govt. solvency and improved gross revenues.
2. Improved profitability of all businesses.
3. Reduced black money.
4. Increased foreign currency holdings.

MBBS will produce four second-order (i.e., medium-term) results:

1. Net surpluses for Govt. and, therefore, more Govt. investment.

2. Cash surpluses for US businesses, which will encourage investment.
3. Eliminate hoarding and increased money liquidity.
4. Reduce dependency on oil money.

MBBS will produce four third-order (i.e., long-term) results:

1. Increased national human productivity and health and reduced levels of unemployment.
2. Increased private investment and the growth of GDP until it sustains acceptable standards of living for all citizens.
3. A free-market economy with few internal/external barriers and tax burdens and a general awareness that government solvency is critical for maintaining the security, welfare, and prosperity of the system and the people of the USA
4. The ability of Govt. and the central bank to plan for future foreign exchange needs, which will stabilize the dollar. These results depend on the ability of MBBS to deliver significantly more cash to Govt. than the current tax system.

MBBS will provide the largest contribution to the revenue system when this system is applied to all economic transactions in the USA's economy. Economic activity usually involves a string of supporting importers, material and equipment suppliers and service companies that form a chain to the manufacturer or provider of goods and services. This activity is also supported downstream by logistics and wholesale distributors. This system is often referred to as the value-added chain because it shows how the value/eventual price of a product or service is built up at each stage.

MBBS, through USMF, would offer to buy the total output from agriculture, manufacturing, and certain services from producers at agreed prices plus 5% in cash or 15% in bonds. People would be encouraged to participate in MBBS because they would be able to take advantage of the duty-free importation of capital, material, and goods.

To estimate the impact of MBBS, a simple model has been developed based on existing data concerning the USA's GDP and how it is broken down. The model assumes that at the first stage of value addition there are activities by importers and suppliers. Thereafter, the core added-value sectors of agriculture, industry, and services are included, followed by distribution.

The model is simplified because the supply chain of some manufacturing and service businesses can be complex. For example, equipment suppliers have a sub chain and distributors who supply factories and offices. Although this chain can be complex, MBBS would produce more revenue as the number of bond transactions increase.

Sustaining the Value of the MBBS Bond

The MBBS bond is intended to have negotiable value throughout its life. While the cost of a bond is determined by the price paid for it, an unused bond also has an open-market value because of the demand for goods and services.

The maintenance of value is critical because it is likely that bond value will fluctuate within reasonable limits. This will encourage people to save bonds in the same way they save shares, savings certificates, and gold and silver.

The MBBS bond would be subject to the following:

1. It would be subject to substantial, continual demand because of the need to sustain economic activity.
2. It would be subject to the maintenance of supply management controls to ensure bonds sustain GDP growth without the danger of inflation.
3. Open-market operations through the USMF agents and private sellers would ensure that buyers/sellers/agents would act in their best interests to maintain a stable, positive market rate.
4. The limited period of cheaper bonds at the beginning of a financial year will ensure a healthy open market when official

channels dry up or become relatively expensive. This alone will keep minimum open market rates above or around five bonds per dollar.

5. It is anticipated that banks and finance houses will purchase large quantities of bonds at the start of each year and hold them for their customers. As a result, a bank's customers would be able to purchase bonds at any time during the year and in large quantities provided they are willing to pay the bank's risk and profit margin.

The Government of USA's MBBS Balance Sheet and Cash Flow

MBBS will produce revenues in the following areas:

1. The sale of Govt. price-controlled goods and services.
2. Operations in USA's added-value chain.
3. The use of MBBS bonds in the retail sector.
4. The use of MBBS as an import agency for goods and services arriving in USA for sale or use in the country.

Table 15 and Figure 12 show how MBBS produces revenues. In some cases, these figures are estimates based on broad economic data, and as such, they are no better and no worse than methods deployed by governments to forecast tax revenues.

It is important to remember that the concession made by Govt. to start MBBS (i.e., reducing the price of controlled items) is more than compensated for by:

1. Reduced Black money (i.e., its migration to the open, lawful economy).
2. Increased USA GDP.

Table 15. The State of Govt.'s Finances in MBCS

Total receipts in billions $						
	Years from MBCS Introduction					
	1	2	3	4	5	Average
Govt.-controlled goods and services	250	300	360	432	518.4	372.08
Receipts from retail markets	75	90	108	129.6	155.5	1115.1
Receipts from industry and commerce	457.125	548.55	658.25	789.25	947.9	6800.35
Total receipts from current activity	782.125	938.505	1126.26	1351.51	1621.815	11640.05
Beneficial receipts from exchange control	60	60	60	60	60	600
Grand Total	842.125	998.55	1186.26	1411.51	1681.815	1224.05
Absorption of black economy %	10	10	10	10	10	10
GDP Growth Forecasts	4	5	6	6	6.5	5.5

Note: This Table does not include the funds and benefits that would result from the Gold Mine, unused money, interest free banking, corporate farming, or foreign investment.
Above are all approximate figures as the exact amount can't be determined till the system is actually implemented for a whole period of at-least 1 year.

Table 15. The State of Govt.'s Finances in MBBS

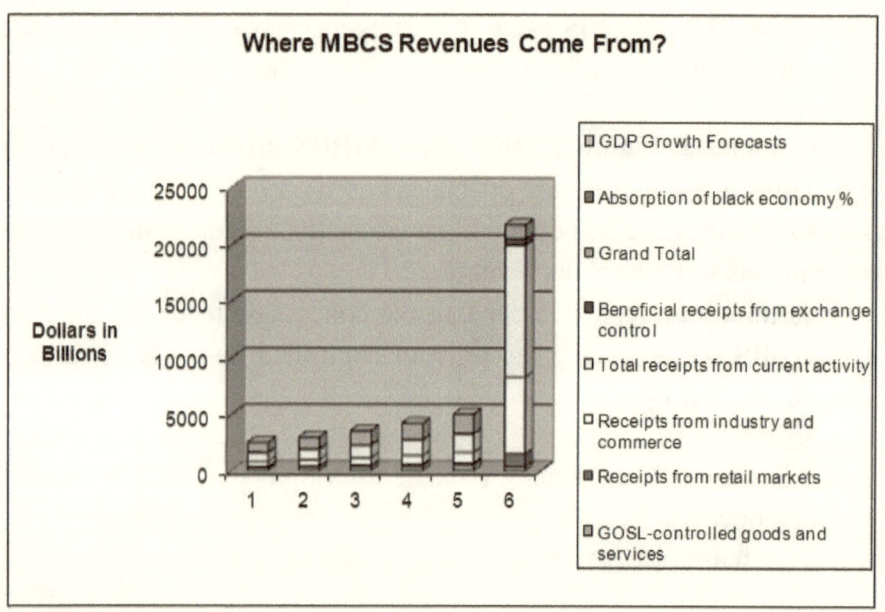

Figure 12. Source of MBBS Revenues

Corporate Farming

In MBBS, Govt. would provide selected corporate farming organizations with up-to-date machinery and equipment, free water, low-cost electricity, and low-cost fuel. Airplanes would be used to spray pesticides and sow seeds. Boundaries would vanish except on paper and in computers, and land could be sold without fear of litigation. The government would share profits with these corporations, which would reduce the subsidies presently paid out by Govt. As a result, every piece of land would be cultivated with high-quality production costs.

Govt. would export these crops and earn much-needed foreign exchange and use corporate farming agencies to sell these crops inside the country. Therefore, the government would be able to easily regulate the price of these crops.

The True Interest Free Banking System

This system serves the same purpose as conventional banking, but it is based on the idea of profit and loss sharing. The Interest free banking system is guided by the concepts of *profit sharing, safekeeping, joint venture, cost plus, leasing.*

In order to avoid charging or paying interest in a mortgage transaction, the interest free banking system uses an approach called *Cost Plus*. A bank may buy a house and sell it to a prospective buyer at a profit or build a house on turnkey basis. The buyer pays for the house in installments. These installments are the actual loan plus rent, which is a percentage of the prevailing interest rate and which is reduced with every installment. A bank may also use an approach called *leasing*. In this approach a bank will sell a vehicle to a buyer in exactly the same way as it will sell a house. The bank's profit is from the rent of the house or car, not from selling it at a higher price to the buyer. This is true interest free banking.

In the *Joint venture* approach, a company repays a bank loan by sharing its profits with the bank. This profit-sharing agreement ends when the loan is repaid.

Using the *profit sharing* approach, a bank and borrower enter into a joint venture. The bank provides venture capital, and the borrower provides the labor. In this way, the bank and borrower share the risk and the profit.

The true form of interest free banking is *partnership* (i.e., sharing, profit and loss), and this will constitute about 90% to 95% of the major business carried out in MBBS. *Profit sharing* and *leasing* will form the basis for the final 5% to 10% of transactions. Once MBBS is implemented, there will be a massive transfer of funds from private accounts. As a result, private banks will depend on government funds to provide money to businesses and industries. Figure 13 illustrates how interest free banking will work in MBBS.

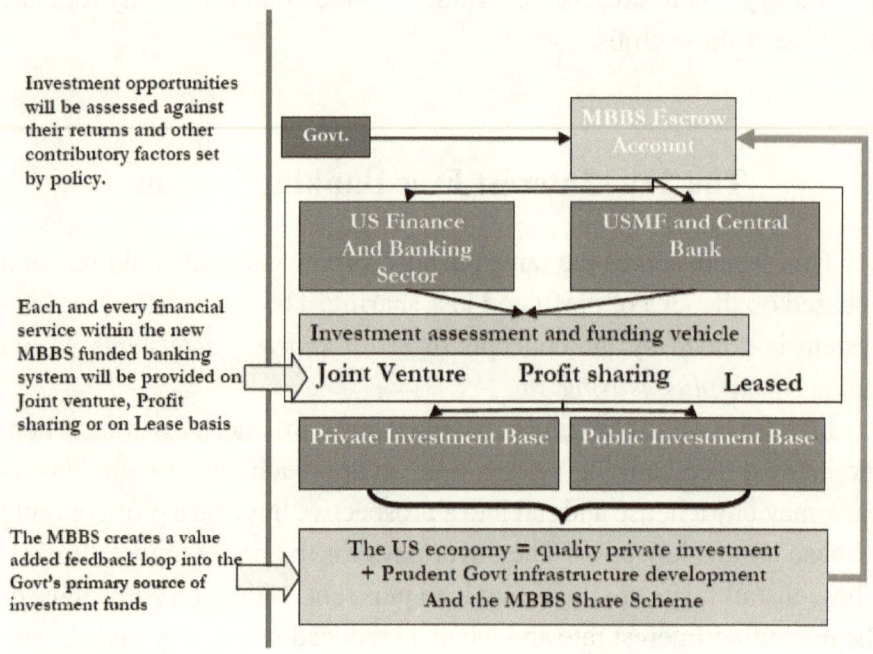

Figure 13. How Interest free Banking works in MBBS

10 FAQ's

- Am I really saving?
- How do I know what I actually pay?
- Where/how do I buy shares?
- How much will I pay for them?
- How do I get the incentives?
- How do the poor manage under this system?
- Will shares be accepted everywhere?
- Can private enterprise enter the scheme?
- Can I buy shares after Q1?
- Will shares be tradable between people, groups and businesses?

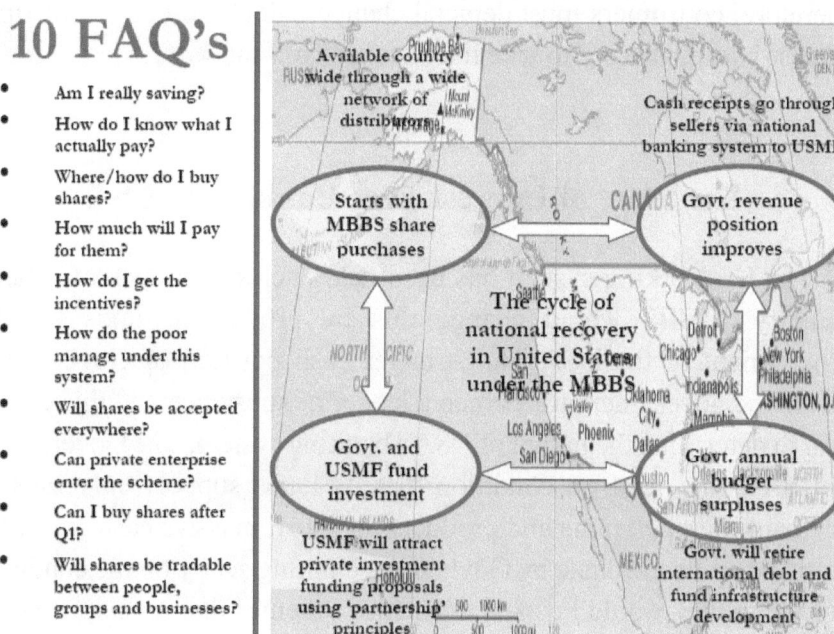

Figure 14. USA's Economic Recovery under MBBS

The key factor for success is Interest free banks' relationship with the depositor. Interest free banking must develop attractive low-, medium- and high-risk investment products. It must issue credit cards in order to compete with other banking systems. In addition, interest free banking must develop acceptable short and medium-term cash flow financing management facilities for businesses and individuals. In short, interest free banks must become credible, respected go-betweens that link investment with opportunity.

Although interest free banks must develop customer services that can compete with interest-based banks, customers also need to become responsible investors. People must be prudent and develop realistic expectations. They must become aware that they have a responsibility to the wider community when they invest. Prudent, responsible investment will help alleviate poverty and ease the burden on people who support the poor. Banks do not own a depositor's money; they just manage it.

Therefore, consumers must demand change before there is a shift from interest-based banking to true interest free banking.

The Start of Interest-Free Banking in USA

The US banking system has been held back by the lack of official liquidity. MBBS would change this by producing funds for the Government of the USA The stronger cash position of Govt. would enable the government to become a lender of substance and this can be used to determine the nature of USA's banking system. The Government of USA could lend on condition that its loans support only interest free banking operations and products. In short, massive cash surpluses would be made available by Govt. to the banking sector on the condition that the money would be used to finance schemes that are approved by appropriate committees.

MBBS would promote interest-free banking because it will reduce the risk of project failure and enable bankers to make more accurate forecasts about project revenues and profits. Figure 15 illustrates the role of banks in MBBS.

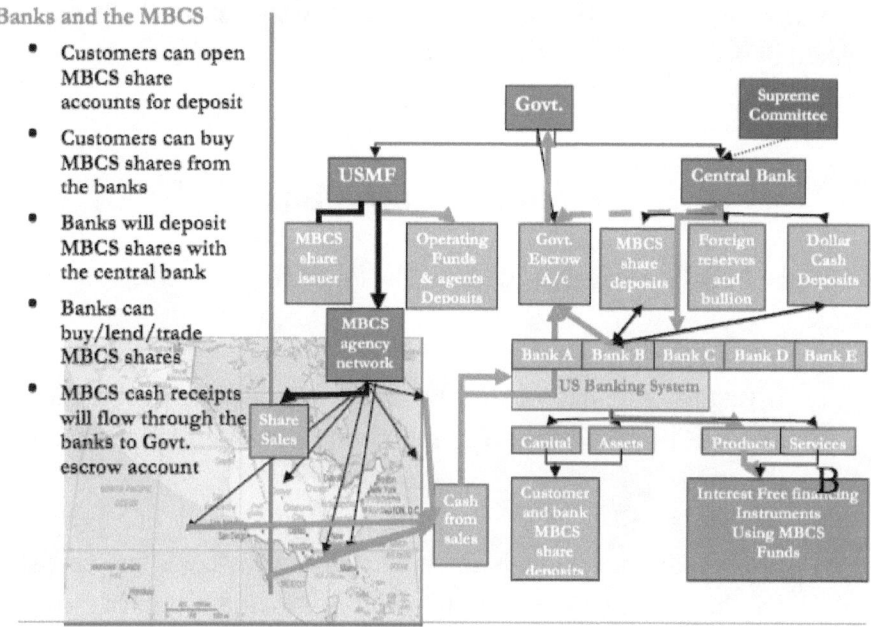

Creating an incentive based economy

Figure 15. Role of Banks in MBBS

Interest-Free Banking

Interest-free banking seems to be impossible because interest has very deep, firm roots in the global marketplace. However, if MBBS totally replaces current tax systems, interest-free banking becomes a real possibility. Once MBBS is fully implemented, money belonging to the private sector held by banks will be transferred to US Government accounts. Once there are few funds available to banks from the private sector, they will have to depend on Govt., which will be more than willing to provide funds, but only on a profit-and-loss sharing basis. Banks will have no option but to take loans from Govt. and invest in the private sector on the same basis, but only after making sure the investment is profitable. Any bank constantly losing money will not be given fresh loans and face being closed down. In MBBS, banks will profit from the hundreds of new businesses and industries that would be created by a dynamic, growing economy.

Role of the Central Bank

Under MBBS, banks would follow the following rules when providing loans:

1. Investors will deposit a 20% down payment as collateral and deposit it in the bank. The remaining 80% will be provided by the state.
2. Investors will have to provide a feasibility study of a proposed project, and it will have to be verified by the bank and certified by the central bank. Govt. will be the final authority on the feasibility of a business or industry.
3. No cash will be advanced until the project is completed (i.e., turn-key basis). This will eliminate the major cause of bad debts.
4. Operating expenses will be paid from the 20% down payment received by the bank. In some cases, the investor may have to put down more than 20% in order to cover operating costs.
5. No other collateral is needed.
6. Bank will employ a team of experts on a commission basis, and they will be paid from the profit according to a pre-agreed contract. In case of loss the team of experts will not receive any commission. Any team repeatedly incurring losses will be blacklisted and will not be able to obtain new contracts. This condition will safeguard the bank from major losses.
7. Any bank constantly showing losses will not be awarded fresh loans and faces going out of business. The chances of bad loan or losses are completely eliminated.
8. The state will not interfere with any business sponsored by it, but the central bank can and will interfere in the case of loss or fraud.

9. The share of the profit will be 40/60, where sate will accept 40%, and the remaining 60% will be divided between the investor and the bank when the bank is a partner with an investor.

10. Investors or a bank can increase their investment up to 60%, and 40% will be invested by the state. In these cases, the profit margin will be 80/20. The state will receive 20%, and the bank and investors will divide the remaining 80%.

11. The distribution of profits between investors and a bank is an internal affair and will not be influenced by the state, but the final contract between the investor and bank will part of the main contract.

12. The state will provide duty-free raw material, machinery and other equipment, electricity, telephone service, fuel and other services below cost. This will increase the profitability of businesses as the production cost for them is reduced. The state will cover the loss incurred by providing below-cost services and recover it from the profit. It is expected that the net income of the state will never be less than 20%, even after providing below-cost services. This incentive will only be given to big businesses, and because the government will be a shareholder in all these businesses, it will realize trillions of dollars in profit every year.

MBBS banking will have some profound effects on the economy:

1. Bankruptcy laws will be eliminated and end the unchecked profit of liquidators, which cause tremendous loss to shareholders and investors. The courts will deal with rare cases of fraud.

2. The state will establish interest free insurance and ensure that the investor is protected from an unexpected loss in case of fire or natural calamities. To insure this loss, the investor has to deposit 5% of the profit in a government account for a time period decided by the investor. If there is no catastrophic event, the state will refund the investor's money minus the profit the state has earned from it. The investor is secured, and the loss is

covered by state. With all these checks and balances, the chances of major loss are less than 0.1%, which can be covered by the profits the government earns from the thousands of investors who participate in this insurance scheme.

The central bank will play an important role in the MBBS banking system. Its experts will check every feasibility study before allowing a bank to go ahead with an investment.

Impact of MBBS on USA's Banks

Interest-free banking will increase banks' profits because hundreds of new businesses and industries will take advantage of the large amount of money available with a 20% down payment as collateral. Banks will also make profits by buying and selling bonds to their bond account holders. Interest based banking will be eliminated because there will be no money available to invest. Even if money were available, it would be impossible to attract people willing to borrow money on an interest basis.

In MBBS, consumers would have only one account, and this account would earn profit on a daily basis. This profit will not be based on interest. Instead, consumers will earn profit on a profit-and-loss sharing basis. Consumers would be able to open a government account or a bank account, and this will be guided by the best rate of return.

Credit cards would be available to consumers, but their spending limit would be restricted to the amount of money they have in a bank account. Every month the profit would be calculated according to the deposits remaining in that account. This will solve the problem of overspending, which is a prevalent problem in developed countries.

Implementing MBBS
The Government of the USA's Role in MBBS

MBBS requires the wholehearted endorsement of the Government of the USA and people must recognize its role as the sponsor of MBBS. Laws must be put in place to establish MBBS and a system for distributing bonds, collecting revenue, and overseeing and administering the scheme. The government would also play a key role in setting policy.

Each year, the Finance Ministry would determine the total bond value and the denominations and terms and conditions for bond use and it would take into account the number of bonds already in circulation. The bonds would have a face value representing dollars, and it would be necessary to exercise monetary controls to prevent inflation and keep the supply within reasonable limits that neither hinder activity nor cause a reduction in a bond's face value. This is already a common part of fiscal policy.

In essence, the government would authorize the issue of bonds at a value approximating the needs of the state budget and the anticipated level of economic activity. As prediction is an art and not a science, budget surpluses and deficits arising from windfalls and shortfalls would have to be managed in the medium to long-term (i.e., through the next year's budget or through emergency mid-term budgets). The government would have to control MBBS policy and strategy, because it is a state revenue system. It would also need to ensure that MBBS remains relevant in concept, objectives, and implementation.

The following criteria will ensure the ongoing success of MBBS:

1. MBBS must be accessible in all parts of the country and for US expatriates abroad.
2. It is necessary for the system to continually make goods and services available at realistic prices.
3. There must be real discounts for using bonds.

If these issues are always addressed, the system will take care of itself because demand for bonds will always exist.

The Implementation Strategy

The following is not intended as an exhaustive description of implementing the system. Instead, only the basic features of implementation are discussed.

Prior to the launch of the scheme, the Government of the USA must tender contracts that cover the following tasks essential to the launch and administration of MBBS:

1. A general management and administration contract.
2. A card/bond design, security, and manufacturing contract.
3. An audit contract.

These contracts will form the structure for MBBS in USA There are certain activities that must be performed in order to make the scheme a success:

o Publicizing and marketing the system throughout the USA.
o Setting up the bond infrastructure (i.e., logistics) so the card/bond system is available throughout the marketing area.
o Printing and manufacturing bonds.
o Entering into contracts with bond vendors.
o Gathering, consolidating, controlling, and accounting for the revenue received from the sale of MBBS card/bonds.

It will be necessary to simplify the administration and revenue-gathering functions in order to ensure MBBS is a success. Therefore, it may be best to assign all of the roles set out above to one particular organization. However, there are also benefits to awarding the above contracts to different, competent organizations in the USA.

It is assumed that a major US bank(s) can play management/administrative roles in the nationwide structure gathering revenues from card/bond sales and consolidating them into a national interest account made available to the government. A bank that administers MBBS will be given a percentage of the net proceeds. This involves no cash outlay by the government. It may be considered prudent to hand the administration of the bond system to the same bank, provided it has a network of branches with access to the anticipated source of revenues. This will ease administration costs and enhance accountability.

In order to make bonds available to the largest number of people, it will be necessary to recruit bond vendors. In order to cover the entire population of the USA, it may be necessary to employ as many as fifty thousand bond vendors in cities, towns, and, in some cases, villages. This would improve the employment situation among the many educated Americans, who are currently unemployed.

Each bond agent will be employed on 10% commission bases, so $100 worth of bonds will be sold for $90. These agents will be registered with the USMF and pay $500 a year, which will be used by the USMF to establish a network of offices and modern communications throughout the country. It is estimated that at least 10,000 offices will be needed to serve the bond agents. Each bond agent will be required to sell $300,000 a month and this can be increased according to demand. An agent who cannot pay the $500 fee will be required to sell $150,000 until he/she is able to pay the registration fee.

Incentive for Multiplication Effect to Investor, Govt. & Poor Population

Investors who purchase $50,000 worth of bonds to sell to people who cannot purchase large quantities of bonds during the discount period (i.e., five bonds per $ during the first month of a financial year) would be able to negotiate a 5% to 7% discount from the bond seller, who would pay this out of his or her 10% commission. The bond seller would be willing to give an investor this discount because the investor would need to purchase large quantities of bonds during the discount period. In this scheme, the investor would sell bonds at the discount rate and keep the 5% to 7% negotiated with the bond seller as profit. As a result, instead of only 5% of the population being able to take advantage of the discount period, at least 50% of the population would be able to take advantage of the low rates available during the discount period. Not only would this benefit large numbers of average people, it would also provide the USMF with more money.

By the end of 30 days of discount period the investor has earned 50%-150% profit depending on his efforts to resell the bonds at Government rates but keeping the share of his profit of 5%-7% which he has negotiated with the bond agent. This will be an open secret and even a non investor will join in this Mega Sale by Hook or Crook (Borrowing from Banks, selling valuables like Gold) or forming teams to collect 50,000 required.

Grassroots Organization

Bond vendors will retain a percentage of all sales. This will be their only form of payment. It is incentive based and promotes far more activity than a government salary.

The use of references, educational requirements (e.g., minimum O level standard), and forms of collateral guarantees will ensure competent people become vendors. Cash deposits may be deemed suitable under the circumstances. Most vendors will be students or unemployed people.

Simplicity is the key to success, but it may be necessary to establish a supervisory level because of the number of card/bond vendors involved in selling MBBS bonds. This supervisory layer should be kept to a minimum so the effectiveness of the card/bond system is not affected and to prevent abuse. Using an existing bank structure/organization appears to be the most logical and expedient method for creating an instant administrative framework. (See Figure 16 for details about the structure of MBBS in the USA)

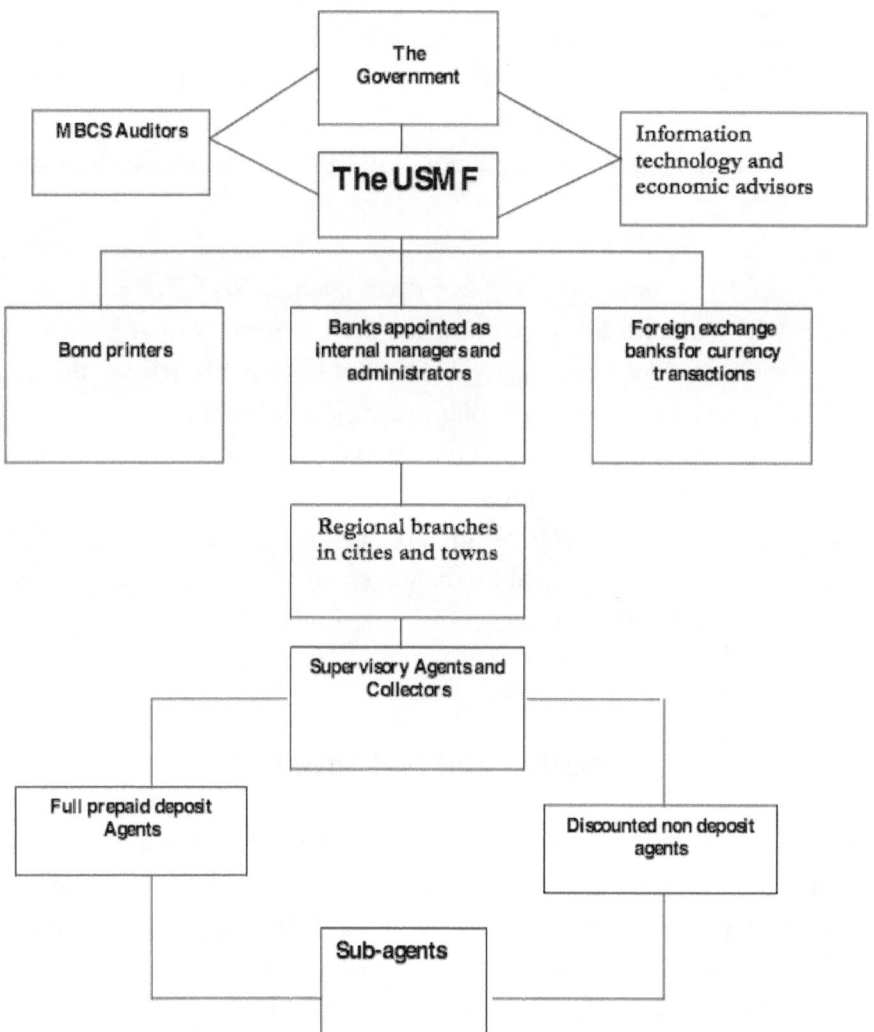

Figure 16. The Proposed Structure of MBBS in USA

A Flood of Money

As mentioned earlier, there is a flood of money waiting to wash into government accounts. This money will come from a number of sources:

1. Massive sale of bonds: It is expected that within one month 25% of the population will buy $3.75 trillion worth of bonds, and its multiplication effect will generate another $3.75 trillion because at least 50% of the population will join in this massive incentive scheme.
2. Gold mine: This is considered the backbone of every country's economy, and it will replace taxes such as VAT. For example, it will generate $100.8 trillion for the USA every year supposing that if total daily transactions across USA is $10 trillion dollars.
3. Interest free banking: The government will be a shareholder in every big business, and the potential revenue generated through this source is unimaginable.
4. Foreign investments: With no tax and low-cost services and commodities provided by the government, it will be difficult for foreign investors to resist investing in the USA.

Deflation and Not Inflation

Once MBBS is implemented, the government will control all imports, exports, agriculture and major businesses. This will eliminate the control of these economic areas by cartels. This will help stop inflation because MBBS will eliminate the price hikes cartels use to improve profits. Without these price hikes, there will be no inflation. Although inflation will be eliminated in MBBS, there is a possibility of deflation. This possibility will exist as long as the government remains true to the incentives that drive MBBS.

Interest Free Instead of all Other Interest Based Financial Instruments

The following criteria must be used to float interest free s (i.e., MBBS bonds):

1. No interest will be paid on these bonds (i.e., bonds).
2. They will not increase the debt burden of the government and should not require any guarantee to print them.
3. Bonds must be available on a supply and demand basis at all times and have no restriction on the amount.
4. Bonds must benefit everybody when used with real currency to purchase goods and services.
5. Bonds cannot be hoarded and should be available from different sources; however, the rate may differ from day to day and from place to place.
6. Everybody must have the opportunity to buy Bonds at the cheapest rate.
7. Buying and selling bonds must occur like any other commodity, but unlike other commodities, these will never be in short supply.
8. Bonds must have an unlimited shelf life.
9. Daily, weekly, or monthly inter bank rates must be based on actual currency but without interest.
10. Bonds must be available to registered businesses at the cheapest rate throughout the year.
11. People must be able to buy Bonds 24 hours a day, 365 days a year.
12. People must be able to buy unlimited amounts of bonds.

MBBS will result in the following benefits for USA and its people:

1. Because of the strong profit incentive, the government will sell bonds worth trillions every year, and there will be massive revenue collection by the government early in the fiscal year and throughout the year.

2. There will be a strong incentive to buy bonds using foreign currency, which will result in large hard currency reserves.
3. There will be daily lotteries to provide average citizens with a chance to share in the profits earned by the government.
4. There will be no kickbacks as is the case in the sale of Euros, which only benefit a few highly placed people.
5. Black money will be used to purchase these bonds. This flood of black money will enable the government to invest in big projects, such as dams to produce electricity and oil/gas field and mineral exploration.
6. All spare and unused money or valuables will be used to buy these bonds for business purposes and reduce the cost of all types of bills and commodities.
7. These bonds will reduce costs at least 10% to 20% from the present price and at least 50% when these bonds are bought at the cheapest rate.
8. The sale of these bonds will provide job opportunities for millions of unemployed, educated people.
9. Bonds can be treated just like money. That is, they can be held in bank accounts and withdrawn through ATM machines.
10. Bonds will be available in the form of debit cards.
11. Even the poorest person should be able to buy and sell bonds at a prompt margin. USA has been used as an example of MBBS because the country is at a crossroads. What is undertaken in the next 3 to 5 years will have a profound effect on the long-term political stability and financial security of the USA and its international prestige. The improvement of the Government of the USA's liquidity is vital to American political stability and financial security. The USA cannot afford more budget deficits. Current levels of Govt. indebtedness require a regular restructuring of external debt as well as massive interest payments.

Many Americans people believe there is fixed or diminishing wealth in USA. The people and government appear to be fighting against this vanishing wealth and taxation is their battleground. This idea is flawed and dangerous because it fails to see the promise of growth held by a solvent government able to build roads, schools, hospitals, ports, airports, and other infrastructure projects, which would inject vital value into the economy and increase the GDP of the USA. In other words, a solvent government will produce a bigger cake for everyone to share.

MBBS provides the US with the opportunity to work its way out of the downward spiral of diminishing value and diminishing tax revenues. By improving the government's ability to collect revenue and spend it wisely, the country's economy can move in a positive direction. In addition, MBBS revenue would increase the growth in GDP. The country could once again pay its way in the world without the need for foreign loans. It is necessary to reverse the USA's downward economic and political spiral and fulfill the expectations of its citizens.

MBBS is a government revenue system that has a wide range of applications to national economies. It is not solely a system for helping developing economies and poorer countries. It can also be used by developed and advanced economies. Indeed, in the fast-growing global marketplace, today's economic giants are being challenged by the Asian tigers, and in order for them to compete. They need to respond in an innovative and responsible way. No economy can rest too comfortably on its past economic performance or its assumptions about the future. In fact, in the new global marketplace, governments need to rethink how they collect and use revenue.

According to Michael Porter of the Harvard University Business School, national economies can be classified using the following four basic characteristics:

1. Factor driven.
2. Diversified production base.
3. Research and development.
4. Wealth driven.

These characteristics show the path from dependence on extraction industries to the achievement of wealth using investments. Of course, all four conditions can co- exist in any economy. However, Porter suggests that an economy's stage of development can be determined by identifying which characteristic dominates an economy.

It is also possible to identify a nation's stage of economic development by examining its citizens' quality of life. The United Nations uses the Human Development Index (HDI) to measure the quality of life in each country. Although HDI uses a broad range of measures, economics is a core measure because the richest nations tend to have the highest HDI scores. Table 16 shows some sample HDI scores.

Table 16. Sample HDI Scores

HDI Rank	Country	Human development index (HDI) value 2014
1	Norway	0.955
2	Iceland	0.906
3	Australia	0.938
4	Luxembourg	0.875
5	Canada	0.911
6	Sweden	0.916
7	Switzerland	0.913
8	Ireland	0.916
9	Belgium	0.897
10	United States	0.937
11	Japan	0.912
12	Netherlands	0.921
13	Finland	0.892
14	Denmark	0.901
15	United Kingdom	0.875
16	France	0.893
17	Austria	0.895

(The 2013/14 Human Development Report by the United Nations Development Program)

HDI measures not only GDP, but also education, health services, literacy, communications, population characteristics, and so forth to obtain a broad assessment of a country's quality of life. Wealth in itself is not enough to assess a country's quality of life; instead, how wealth is used is a key factor in measuring the relative development of a country. In addition, it is necessary to examine a country's tax system and how it affects that country's development. The tax systems used in developed countries do not appear to have a negative effect on quality of life, but in spite of appearances, MBBS could improve life in developed countries faster than their current tax systems.

CHAPTER THREE

CONCLUSION

The mutual benefit bond system (MBBS) is based on incentive-based principles that prohibit interest and taxes. Interest and taxes have driven most of the world's population into poverty and MBBS eliminates these two evils and offers the best hope for eliminating poverty in the shortest period of time. Most non-Muslim countries might consider MBBS a tool to spread Islam. As a result, they may be hesitant to implement MBBS. However, they will have no chance for survival if other countries implement it. The country that implements MBBS first will become an economic leader.

In order to raise enough money to meet national budgets, it is necessary to use a system of revenue collection that encourages people to participate in the scheme and produces large amounts of cash for a government quickly and at no extra cost or risk. The mutual benefit bond/card system is an incentive-based revenue system that replaces current tax systems and encourages people to invest in their countries.

MBBS is:

1. Eliminate unfair financial burdens from all sectors of society.
2. Remove taxes, duties, and levies.
3. Revolutionize government revenue collection and liquidity.
4. Eliminate poverty.
5. Rebuild national infrastructures.
6. Restore law and order.
7. Provide all citizens with equal opportunities.

MBBS is a very simple system. There are no checks and balances, hardly any documentation compared to the documentation in existing systems, and no chance of corruption. In addition, there is zero risk to existing government systems that generate revenue.

MBBS is easy to implement. It would be easy to find enough people willing to work for a MBBS agency, and all bond vender positions would be filled in weeks. A country's treasury would print bonds instead of currency. A monetary agency could be set up in one week. As a result of the large amount of money bonds vendors would make, it would take the monetary agency little time to establish its network, and this network would not cost the government any money. Given the benefits of MBBS, it would not be difficult to pass the legislation needed to implement the system.

No country can survive without implementing MBBS because this system will eliminate poverty, create massive employment, create an industrial revolution, improve law and order, eliminate drug-related problems and crimes, and eliminate the terrorism that is fueled by poverty. Any country that does not implement MBBS would face a public revolt and would be replaced by a government willing to implement this system.

A world without interest payments, poverty, and taxes, a world where law and order are the norm and a person has the opportunity to reach his or her potential on a level playing field would be a paradise to most people, but this paradise seems like a pipe dream, an illusion. It seems like an impossible dream to find a system that would eliminate interest payments and taxes and at the same time, improve people's quality of life and enable them to reach their potential. However, using the mutual benefit bond system, it is possible to create a world that is free of interest payments, poverty and taxes. With MBBS, it is possible to create a paradise on Earth.

CHAPTER FOUR

FREQUENTLY ASKED QUESTIONS

What is a MBBS bond?

A MBBS bond can be viewed as a mandatory payment for goods and services. The bearer of these bonds would be entitled to significant formularized discounts on the listed sale price/cost of goods and services if these bonds are used with a cash payment. In the government sector, a consumer can pay in bonds instead of cash, and the bonds will be worth double the amount of currency. In the private sector, goods and services would be purchased with 15% in bonds and the rest in cash.

How can these bonds be used? What are the benefits of using these bonds?

These bonds would be used to obtain reduced prices for goods and services offered by the government and the public sector. These bonds will bring down the cost of living for a household consumer and reduce production costs for businesses.

Who will sell MBBS bonds, and who will be eligible to sell bonds?

Unemployed and preferably educated people would be hired as MBBS agents. These people would have, at least, matriculated. They would be required to register with the USMF for an annual fee of US$500. The USMF would conduct an intensive, but short training course and it would offer a 10% discount to agents and assigned them a monthly quota of bonds worth US$300,000, which would enable a bond agent to earn up to US$30,000 a month.

What if a person cannot pay the US$500 registration fee?

If a person cannot pay the US$500 registration fee, then his or her monthly quota will be reduced by 50% until the agent has paid the full registration fee.

How do you control the artificially raised prices and subsidized prices of the commodities/services produced by private sector?

MBBS does not control the prices of the private sector; instead, it helps control prices by reducing the cost of production by at least 50% and eliminating taxes and import duties. Therefore, there is no artificial price or overprice in the private sector, and each product or service will be cheaper than the artificial price if the consumer uses 15% in bonds and the rest in cash.

Why pay for expenses that will be incurred in the future?

Purchasing bonds for future purchases will ensure that the consumer pays reduced prices because the bonds are inexpensive and will buy products and services with reduced prices.

Is there any financial incentive for this advance payment other than bonds?

No, there is no other financial incentive, and the consumer would get bonds according to the prescribed sliding scale. However, consumers who buy bonds during the discount period would receive more bonds for their money and be entitled to waivers for import duties. In addition, they would be able to sell bonds at a profit when the cost of bonds increases later in a financial year.

Does the purchase of US$50,000 worth of bonds entitle the consumer to any duty-free imports?

A person or business that purchases US$50,000 worth of bonds in the first month of a financial year is entitled to import US$500,000 worth of goods and services duty free.

How will the government control the under-invoicing of goods and services?

People under-invoice in order to evade duties and taxes. There will be no need to under-invoice when custom duties are partially or completely waived.

People who invest US$50,000 receive extra bonds, or they have the option to import goods and services duty free. However, people who invest less do not receive these benefits. Why?

Incentives such as extra bonds or a waiver of duties are available to people spending US$ 50,000. Although some people cannot buy this many bonds on their own, groups of low-income people can combine their funds and buy low-cost bonds. Even if they cannot raise enough money to buy large amounts of bonds, they will still receive a 30% to 60% reduction in their cost of living when they use their bonds. In addition, a rich or clever businessperson can buy low-cost bonds and negotiate a 4% to 8% discount from a bond agent. He or she would be able to sell these bonds at the lowest rate to people who are unable to raise US$ 50,000 and retain the discount as profit. This process can be repeated throughout the first month and result in high profits for the seller and low rates for the buyer.

How can a government generate the same amount of revenue in subsequent years if bonds are valid indefinitely and are in circulation right from the very first day?

The use of bonds is not restricted to individual consumers. Traders, manufacturers, importers, agriculturists, and corporate entities will also require bonds for their day-to-day use. These bond users will buy and sell their merchandise through the United States Monetary Fund (USMF). Spare bonds can be sold on the open market at a profit or surrendered to the government to obtain duty-free options.

The use of black money in this system will not generate the same amount of revenue in subsequent years. What remedies are available to the government?

The government will invest black money or extra cash in high-tech companies, big business, and land reforms and it will receive a profit from these investments every year. Therefore, the government will not have any need for black money after the first year.

What is the organizational structure of the USMF? How does it operate?

The USMF will be a private organization selected by an open-bidding process. It will be responsible for selling bonds through agents, collecting funds from agents, and depositing these funds in government accounts. The USMF will operate regional offices, which will monitor branch offices in each city in their region. These branch offices will be linked by the latest information technology and will be located in the smallest village.

How will the USMF ensure transparent operations?

In order to ensure the USMF's operations are transparent, the next three lowest bidders will be appointed auditors for a fixed fee. In addition, in the case of fraud or mistakes, these auditors will receive 50% of any penalties (i.e., 10 times the amount involved) imposed on the USMF. The government will be the fourth auditor.

Why will the USMF need 100,000 offices with 500,000 employees?

These offices and employees will be administrative in nature, which will ensure smooth, transparent operations, and they will be responsible for maintaining a record of bond sales. In addition, they will dispense bonds to bonds agents.

How will the USMF monitor sales and control revenue collection from bond agents?

Each agent will have a monthly quota of 300,000 bonds. No agent can sell bonds beyond his or her quota. This will ensure that each agent has the same opportunities, and each agent would be able to earn up to US$30,000 a month.

How would the USMF eliminate or minimize the chances of bond agents committing fraud?

All USMF records will be computerized, and a record for each agent will be maintained, which will reduce the chance of fraud or error. Any fraud or complaint against any agent will result in the termination of his or her services. The profits from fraud will be small, so most agents will not jeopardize their jobs for small payoffs.

Currency is supported and backed by reserves. What supports or backs MBBS bonds?

Bonds do not need to be supported or backed by reserve currency, because they can only be bought with actual currency, if a person does not have the money, he or she will not be able to purchase any bonds.

Who will print MBBS bonds and how will they be kept secure?

The government will print MBBS bonds using the same infrastructure, standards, and security measures used to print present currency notes. Large amounts will be available as debit cards.

What will be the size, color and denominations of MBBS bonds?

MBBS bonds will be in the form of debt cards. Their denominations will vary from 1 bond to 5,000 bonds. At later stages, MBBS can be issued in plastic card form similar to credit/debit cards.

What will it cost to print MBBS bonds?

Compared to the revenue generated by MBBS, the cost of printing is negligible and the only expense will be the paper or cards because this system will use the staff and equipment now used to print currency.

The system looks very complicated and hardly possible to implement. Is this true?

MBBS might seem complicated, but even people with limited education can understand it because it only involves two equations and is far simpler than the present tax system, which is only possible to understand with the help of tax consultants. In addition, the money system has been shifted from a binary system to the decimal system, which is considered difficult to understand and implement and used by very few people. Also, bonds agents will educate people about the system.

Will MBBS radically change United States' taxation system?

There will be no change in the tax structure (i.e., direct taxation), until and unless the government is able to meet it revenue needs using MBBS. Until that time, the tax system will remain intact. In addition, there will be no change in indirect taxation. However, MBBS bonds will eventually be the only indirect taxation.

Is there a time limit on the waiver in custom duty?

The waiver of duty will be offered for a limited period of time. After a concessionary period, this waiver will not be available, and the person or business will be subject to the present duty structure. Category 3 businesses that sell their products through the USMF will be able to import duty-free goods or services equal to the amount sold through the USMF throughout the year.

How will this system help alleviate poverty?

This system will bring down the cost of living, and the necessities of life will be available for 30% to 60% less than current market prices. In addition, this system will promote the creation of new industries and increased production in existing industries, which will increase the number of available jobs. This will definitely help reduce poverty in the United States. In a very first week, all unemployed people will be able to get job as a bond agent and earn a decent living at no cost to the government.

How can a poor person obtain bonds at the lowest rates?

Groups of low-income people can combine their funds and buy low-cost bonds during the discount period. In addition, for a security deposit of US$100, a person can buy bonds throughout the year for at least four bonds per dollar in the open market or through the bank by agreement at the start of the system.

Will MBBS create real economic activity?

Yes. MBBS will produce an industrial boom because there will be no tax, no duty, and production costs will be reduced by 50%. This will create jobs and increase exports and reduce imports. With state offering to provide 80% cash to all big businesses on profit and loss sharing basis and major portion (60%) of the profit going to private investors there will be big boom in the industrial sector which is the back bone of the economy.

How will MBBS affect industry in United States?

The United States could be an economic giant if its socioeconomic constraints are removed. MBBS will remove these constraints and enable high-tech industries to grow. This growth in industries will reverse the United States' trade imbalance.

What benefits or incentives are available to a person spending US$100,000 to purchase bonds in the first month of a financial year?

A person spending US$50,000 to purchase bonds in the first month of a financial year will be having following benefits: (1) If a person does not want bonds, he or she can receive a waiver of US$500,000 on import duties for any legal imports, depending on the market rate of goods; (2) they can use a mixture of bonds and waivers (e.g., 125,000 bonds and a waiver of US$250,000 on import duty); (3) they can receive 500,000 bonds for routine bills throughout the year; (4) they can sell bonds for a profit at later stages once the concessionary period lapses; and (5) they can enter a draw for US$ 1 billion, which will be held daily throughout the year.

What is the life of bonds? Do bonds have a due date?

There is no due date, compulsory period of use or expiry date for MBBS bonds. All bonds will have an unlimited life and will continue in circulation in the same way currency circulates.

What will the government do if the value of bonds drops to more than US$5?

The Government of United States will intervene and buy back bonds at a cheaper price 5.5 per dollar and raise the price of bonds. This will not happen because bonds can be surrendered for a duty-free option, provided 50,000 bonds are surrendered.

What effect will MBBS have on real estate?

MBBS will likely crash the real estate market because the profit margin for bonds will be much higher than the profit margin for property. Therefore, it will be cheaper to build a house than buy one. It is estimated that it would could 50% less to build a house under MBBS.

How will MBBS affect the stock market?

Initially, MBBS will crash the stock market. However, it will recover and rise to new heights as a result of the elimination of taxes and a decrease in the price of government-controlled essential goods. Ultimately, the stock market will cease to exist because it is a form of gambling, and investing in bonds carries almost no risk.

Does implementing MBBS pose any risks to the government?

MBBS is a unique, risk-free approach to revolutionizing the collection of government revenue. It does not require giving up current taxes until the system produces enough money to fund government activities. After that, MBBS will transform the United States into an open, transparent, free market where the government and citizens co-operate to drive prices down, create balanced budgets and increase general investment. Therefore, there is absolutely no risk to the government.

When will the government declare a tax-free holiday?

Once the government has collected enough revenue, it will remove all taxes. This will further decrease prices. It is expected that the government will collect more than US$2 trillion in the first week of a financial year because of the incentives offered by MBBS, especially to people holding black money, which will be the main source of revenue collected in the first month.

This system does not provide everyone with equal incentives. Why?

The system is designed to provide financial incentives to everyone. Everyone will receive lower prices when using bonds and cash to purchase goods and services. The lower income population will also get the benefit of a 60% reduction in prices of all goods and services but may be little less than a well to do person because of the open market price may be four or above during the last period of the year. MBBS is not suppose to provide luxury items to every body and it will depend on the earning of the individual.

IMF puts many types of pressure on developing countries. How will a country that implements MBBS deal with these pressures?

At present, these governments are forced to borrow short-, medium- and long- term loans from IMF in order to finance cash imbalances, unplanned shortfalls in tax revenue, and infrastructure development. MBBS will create a positive cash flow for all these government and lead to actual cash surpluses, which will eliminate the need to borrow money and make it possible to repay current loans with interest.

How will MBBS help establish Interest-Free banking?

The government must abandon all interest operations and use its cash surpluses from MBBS to promote investment through co-operation and partnership with the private sector. It would use surplus cash to establish and strengthen an Interest-Free financing system. The government would provide cash needed to finance this banking system.

How will MBBS support Interest-Free banking operations?

The banks in the United States will offer MBBS bond accounts. The banks would have to establish special mandatory bond deposits. They would become as important a seller of bonds as USMF. All investment in the private sector would be done through banks, with 80% of the cash provided by the government and 20% provided by the investor.

The bank would be responsible for overseeing the business, and the government would provide all commodities and services below cost when the government is a partner in the business. The government would receive 40% of the profit, and 60% would be divided by the bank and investor. The state bank would oversee the whole lending process.

People and organizations may hold more bonds than required. Is not hoarding forbidden by the society?

In a society, hoarding is not allowed because of its practical effects on the supply of critical items such as grain, water, and so forth. In MBBS, people would not be able to exercise monopolistic powers because bonds would be freely available from the USMF agents and private sellers. In addition, the central bank could intervene if banks try to manipulate bond rates. In this system, hoarding is not possible because bonds would always be available from the government and the private sector.

Will MBBS isolate United States in international market? How will the government deal with imports and determine business relations with other countries under this system?

MBBS is an internal system and imports and business relationship with other countries will continue in the same way they do today. The only thing that will change is the waiver of duties under certain conditions, which has nothing to do with exporting countries.

How does MBBS compensate the government for the loss of revenue from reduced prices for commodities and the waiver of duties?

The sale of MBBS bonds would more than compensate for the loss of revenue from reduced prices for commodities and the elimination of duties. In fact, the revenue generated by MBBS would many times the amount of money collected from the sale of commodities and duties in whole year.

What is the benefit of bonds to the general public?

Bonds would reduce the price of every commodity or service provided by the government and they would reduce the prices of goods and services provided by the private sector by 40% to 60%.

How will it be possible for the government to collect US$1.5 trillion within a week of a financial year?

According to conservative estimates, 15% of United States' population (i.e., 15 million people) would be willing to spend US$100,000 in order to reduce their cost of living by 40% to 60% and this would generate more than US$1.5 trillion (e.g., US$100,000 x 15 million = US$1.5 trillion). The remaining 90% of the population would also use this system and generate even more money. Moreover, people would purchase large number of bond in order to participate in draw worth US$1 billion that will be held daily throughout the year. Therefore, the government will raise more than US$1.5 trillion in the first month and five times this amount by the end of year.

How does this system support foreign trade?

As discussed above, MBBS reduces production and business costs by 50%. In such conditions, industrialists will have better opportunities for setting up new units or expanding/modernizing existing units. The low cost of manufacturing will make United States' products very competitive on the international market. Very good quality products produced by hi-tech machinery and low prices will boost exports and domestic consumption, and consequently, imports would be reduced and the US trade imbalance would improve.

Does this system benefit government employees?

MBBS would generate large amounts of money for the government, and as a result, the government would be able to improve its salary structure (i.e., increase salaries by at least three times present rates). This increase in salaries would improve the financial situation of employees, which, at present, makes them susceptible to corruption. Therefore, the level of corruption among government employees would decrease.

What is the incentive for people with black money to participate in MBBS?

MBBS would enable people with black money to enter the legitimate economy and import goods duty free and sell these goods through the

USMF. This would double their profits and eliminate the risks associated with smuggling.

Why sell certificates when selling MBBS bonds will generate more money?

In 2009, the Government of United States printed 1 trillion certificates and offered them at an interest rate of less than 1% and this has increased the internal debt of United States. MBBS bonds would generate all the money needed by the government and would not increase the government's internal debt or external debt.

How will MBBS help a business that does not deal with customers?

This type of business can pay a registration fee of US$100,000 and buy bonds every month at five bonds per dollar. This business can get 500,000 bonds for only US$100,000. The higher the registration fee, the more cheap bonds a business can purchase. The only condition is that the business must produce evidence of business operations and prove the registration fee has been paid. More than one business can pool their resources to take advantage of these cheap bonds.

How will MBBS help a business dealing with customers?

This type of business can pay a registration fee that is not less than US$10,000. They can buy twice the amount of bonds collected from customers. For example, with a registration fee of US$10,000, a business can collect up to 10,000 bonds a month and buy 20,000 bonds at a cost of US $3,333, while collected bonds will be replaced without any cost with new bonds. The collection of bonds will be according to the business' annual fee as shown in the bond table. With a registration fee of US$100,000, a business can collect 100,000 shares and buy three times the amount of collected shares at the rate of five bonds per dollar. The higher the registration fee, the more bonds a business can purchase at the cheapest rate. A shopkeeper would be eager to sell his or her merchandise for bonds plus cash. The amount of bonds accepted by a shopkeeper would depend on his or her needs. On the other hand, a customer would be more than happy to purchase merchandise with the help of bonds because bonds would reduce the price of merchandise, because they have been purchased at a reduced rate.

How will MBBS affect the cost of living?

The cost of living will decrease as a result of the elimination of taxes, 50% decrease in the cost of goods and services, and pay raises.

Will MBBS create inflation? Will people buy more goods and services than they need?

MBBS will not create inflation because this system will result in a decrease in prices. It is true that with MBBS people will have more money to buy more goods and services, but that does not mean they will buy more than they need to improve their standard of living.

How will MBBS help low-income people?

Any person who uses government goods or services (e.g., traveling by railway) can use MBBS bonds to obtain substantial discounts. For example, a railway ticket from New York to Los Angeles may cost 400 dollars. In MBBS, the ticket may cost 800 bonds if the bonds are purchased for five bonds per dollar, then the ticket will cost two thirds less than the cost to purchase a ticket using dollars. With bonds, a person will be able to save 40% to 70% on government-controlled goods and services, depending on the rate for bonds.

What is the cheapest price a person or business will be able to pay for MBBS bonds?

Bonds can be purchased for 20 cents per bond, but this rate will only be available in the first month of a financial year or if the buyer has a special registration arrangement with the USMF.

It has been suggested that MBBS can operate at the same time as a current tax system. How will this work if people have to operate under existing tax laws?

It would be necessary to enact legislation that safeguards the interests of a person using bonds, and the government would not question a person's source of income.

Has MBBS been used by any country?

To the best of our knowledge, no country has used MBBS to generate revenue.

How will MBBS affect the fabric of our institutional makeup in terms of conceding power, authority and so forth? How long would it take to be universally accepted and agreed?

Authority tends to corrupt, and absolute authority corrupts absolutely. A large amount of time would have to be devoted to not antagonizing people in power. This is why the USMF would be an autonomous institution. As soon as the United States becomes economically self-sufficient and debt free, MBBS will spread like wild fire.

It seems unrealistic to predict that MBBS will solve United States' revenue problems in 30 days. Is it not true that a project of this magnitude can easily take a few years to implement?

It can take only 30 days to implement this system because of massive incentives for every body.

No marketing and advertising expenses have been mentioned during the discussion about MBBS. Why?

The five million bond agents would educate the public about the benefits of using MBBS bonds. In addition, all the expenses will be paid by the USMF, because of massive revenue has been generated through the registration of bonds agents and the percentage of each bond sold in the market.